My Years in
THERESIENSTADT

My Years in THERESIENSTADT

HOW ONE WOMAN SURVIVED THE HOLOCAUST

Gerty Spies

TRANSLATED BY
JUTTA R. TRAGNITZ

 **Prometheus Books**
59 John Glenn Drive
Amherst, New York 14228-2197

The essays "For Elsa Bernstein, the Person and the Poet, in Memoriam" and "Memories of Dr. Julius Spanier" have been published in the book *Vergangene Tage. Jüdische Kultur in München*, edited by Hans Lamm, 1981. We thank the publishing house Albert Langen-Müller, Munich, for permission to reprint them.

Published 1997 by Prometheus Books

01 00 99 98 97   5 4 3 2 1

Library of Congress Cataloging-in-Publication Data

Spies, Gerty, 1897–
    [Drei Jahre Theresienstadt. English]
    My years in Theresienstadt : how one woman survived the Holocaust / Gerty Spies ; translated by Jutta R. Tragnitz.
        p.   cm.
    Includes bibliographical references.
    ISBN 1–57392–141–6 (cloth : alk. paper)
    1. Spies, Gerty, 1897–   . 2. Theresienstadt (Concentration camp)—Biography. 3. Holocaust, Jewish (1939–1945)—Germany—Personal narratives. 4. Holocaust, Jewish (1939–1945)—Czechoslovakia—Personal narratives. 5. Jewish authors—Germany—Biography. 6. Germany—Ethnic relations. I. Title.
D805.C9Z8813   1997
946.53'18'092—dc21
[B]   97–271
                                                                                    CIP

Printed in the United States of America on acid-free paper

Contents

My Years in Theresienstadt

Acknowledgments

I would like to take this opportunity to thank my many friends who were kind enough to give generously of their time for their support of this project. Without their help this translation would not have been possible. Professor Esther Parada brought Gerty Spies's book to my attention; Helma Mirus assisted my research in Munich; Eva Borowietz helped with biographical data and arranged my visit with Gerty Spies in February 1995; and Mamie Gray rescued me from many computer-related difficulties.

I am greatly indebted to my friends Sari Isaacson and Mary Rosner who read my early manuscript and whose pertinent questions helped me in clarifying significant issues for other readers. My special gratitude goes to Professor Marian Sperberg-McQueen for taking time to carefully read Gerty

7

Spies's book in German simultaneously with an early draft of my translation. Our discussions of particularly demanding passages proved invaluable to my progress with this work, as did her kind words of encouragement. As always, Professor Marvin Mirsky was available whenever I needed help, and his recommendations influenced the final version of my translation. But most of all, I would like to thank my husband, Bob, for his support, understanding, and patience. It takes the concerted effort of many people to bring this kind of labor of love to completion.

Jutta Tragnitz

Introduction

Personal accounts of the Holocaust are painful to read. At the same time these documents often attest to the inner strength and dignity of spirit of which human beings are capable under the most extreme circumstances. This book, *My Years in Theresienstadt,* is one woman's account of her personal struggle for survival and her victory over a system of evil.

Gerty Spies was born in Trier in 1897 into a Jewish family whose ancestors had lived in Germany for centuries. She may have inherited her poetic talent from her father, Sigmund Gumprich, a successful merchant and poet who wrote in the Trier dialect. Her mother had been a nurse. Spies had a close relationship with her two-years-older brother, Rudi, and recalls spending a happy childhood with her family in

Trier. Rudi volunteered in World War I and died shortly before the armistice in 1918.

Spies is very reticent about details of her personal life up to her deportation to Theresienstadt in 1942; much of the information offered here has been gathered from books, newspaper articles, and my correspondence with Spies's friends and relatives; efforts to have Spies herself confirm or expand on the information met with gentle but firm rebuffs. Apparently Gerty Spies graduated from a lyceum in Trier and a year later passed an examination to become a teacher of home economics. After her brother's death she decided to stay home with her parents. In 1920, she married Alfred Spies, a Gentile; the couple moved to Freiburg im Breisgau. Two children were born: a daughter, Ruth (1921–1964), and a son, Wolfgang (1923–).* The marriage ended in divorce in 1927. In 1929, after her father's death, she moved with her mother and daughter to Munich. According to a newspaper article of 1987, her son, Wolfgang, after contracting meningitis, has lived for decades in an institution. Gerty Spies refers to his illness in her book when she recounts her interrogation in Theresienstadt by an SS official about her children (182).

Because of Spies's marriage to a non-Jew and because of her two half-Jewish children, she was spared persecution during the early years of Nazi rule in Germany. She was active in Jewish community organizations and in a Jewish home for children, where part of her task was to prepare her young charges for upcoming transports to concentration

---

*As of publication, Wolfgang is still living.

camps. After a change in the Nuremberg race laws concerning mixed marriages, Spies received her own orders for deportation to Theresienstadt in July 1942, an event recounted in her memoirs. Her young daughter, Ruth, because she was considered half-Jewish, was allowed to finish high school in Munich. She was spared deportation and lived on the outskirts of Munich during the war.

After the liberation of Theresienstadt in May 1945, Spies returned to Munich, and after her reunion with her daughter and a young granddaughter, decided to stay in Germany. In 1949, her daughter emigrated with her family to America, where she died in 1963, according to Spies, "from homesickness" (p. 33). Spies's mother, who had emigrated to America during the 1930s, returned in 1953 and lived with Spies until her death at age ninety-nine.

In 1947, two years after her return to Munich, Gerty Spies published her first book of poetry, *Theresienstadt*. Three more books followed. *Drei Jahre Theresienstadt* (My Years in Theresienstadt), a mixture of prose, diary entries, and verse, was published in 1984. Her next book, *Im Staube gefunden* (Found in the Dust), was published in 1987 and contains poetry not published before. *Das schwarze Kleid* (The Black Dress), from 1992, recalls the changing vagaries of a black dress standing in as a metaphor for the fate of its many owners in Theresienstadt. In 1993, another anthology of poetry, *Gedichte* (Poems), followed.

In the years following the war, Gerty Spies never tired of promoting better understanding and reconciliation between Christians and Jews. She was active in the cultural and literary circles of Munich, giving lectures as well as giving poetry readings from her own works. In 1986, she received the *Schwabinger Kunstpreis für Literatur* (a prize for literature awarded by Schwabing, a district of Munich). In the same year, Spies was elected honorary chairperson of the Society for Christian-Jewish Cooperation. Richard Weiszäcker, president of the German Federal Republic, awarded Gerty Spies the *Bundesverdienstkreuz* in 1987 for her efforts to establish an ongoing dialogue between Jews and non-Jews in Germany. With the exception of the three years of her deportation to Theresienstadt, she lived most of her life in the same apartment in Schwabing, the artists' district of Munich. In 1993, she moved to a senior citizens home on the outskirts of Munich, where in January 1997, Gerty Spies celebrated another birthday, passing the century mark.

Theresienstadt, where Spies was interned, was an atypical concentration camp. It was publicized as a retirement city, a *Vorzugslager,* a place for privileged and prominent Jews to sit out the war. In reality, it was a collection point, a *Schleuse* or sluice, for arriving and departing transports, most of them destined for Auschwitz. As Ruth Schwertfeger, a scholar on women's Holocaust poetry, explains in her book *Women of Theresienstadt,* it was designed "as a camouflage both to divert elsewhere growing world attention to the existence of death camps and to provide a temporary, practical means of disposing of prominent European Jews, mostly from Germany, Austria and Czechoslovakia, who had distinguished themselves in industry, the armed forces or the arts and culture" (69).

Theresienstadt is situated about forty miles northwest of

Prague at the confluence of the rivers Elbe and Eger, surrounded by the central Bohemian mountains. Before World War II, about five thousand people lived in this small fortress city originally built in 1780 by Emperor Franz Joseph II in memory of his mother, Empress Maria Theresa. Later it was converted into a garrison town, and about one kilometer away a smaller fortress was built as a prison with a yard for firing squads and gallows. In November 1941, the original inhabitants were removed, and the city was converted into a kind of hybrid ghetto/extermination camp, housing as many as 60,000 people at one time, most of them, but not all, according to Spies, Jews. H. C. Adler, whose book *Theresienstadt 1941–1945* is considered the definitive account, states that between 1941 and 1945 about 141,000 people went through Theresienstadt. Estimates vary, but it is clear that an overwhelming number of prisoners were women. According to Adler, for every 1,000 male workers there were 1,218 female workers. Furthermore, close to 10,000 children were moved through Theresienstadt. About 33,000 people died there of disease and malnutrition, while about 88,000 prisoners were transported to other camps, primarily to Auschwitz. In May of 1945, 17,000 people were liberated; of these, fewer than 100 were children (Adler, 48, 416, 572).

Since the authorities wanted Theresienstadt to be seen by the outside world as a "model" ghetto, they used the prisoners' artistic activities for their own purposes. In an attempt to divert criticism from neutral foreign states, they encouraged, indeed, even demanded, certain artistic activities within specific guidelines. Arno Parik, in "Art in the Terezin Ghetto," relates that the Nazi government even supervised the production of a movie, giving it the title *The Führer Gives a City to the Jews* (Parik, 54). For propaganda purposes, visiting commissions were allowed to come through: the International Red Cross visited Theresienstadt in June of 1944. Gerty Spies tells of a beautification project, the construction of a sort of Potemkin village. Artists were instructed to paint street scenes depicting "typical" life in Theresienstadt to be hung in the newly refurbished Café. The town square was covered with flower beds and sand paths. Playgrounds were built, and buildings along a selected route were painted and refurbished, at least on the first floor. Storefronts with display windows were set up full of merchandise that had not been seen anywhere in camp before and which remained beyond the reach of prisoners.

The Nazis allowed an ostensibly self-governing body to be set up in Theresienstadt, the Jewish Council of Elders, which nevertheless remained in all matters of importance dependent on the administration of the camp SS Komandantur. This council met in the Magdeburg barracks, to which Spies refers often in her memoirs. This Council of Elders established a "Cultural Department for the Administration of Free Time Activities" to supervise lectures, poetry readings, music recitals, operas and plays, and other artistic activities, including "variety evenings." Though some of the performances had to be pre-approved, many were improvised on the spot and all were well attended.

Jana Sedova writes of her experience with theater performances in Theresienstadt in *Terezin*, a collection of essays written by survivors and published by the Council of Jewish Communities in the Czech Lands in 1965. According to Sedova, the first festive night of theater and cabaret took place in 1942. It was organized and put on by men, and though "the rumor about the success ... penetrated through the thick walls of the barracks into the women's prison ..., the [men's] Sudeten barracks, only a few blocks away [from the women's Dresden barracks] were as inaccessible for us women at that time, as if they had been situated at the other end of the world" (*Terezin*, Sedova, 219). Sedova concludes that "there was nothing left for us to do, but to start our own, purely 'feminine' culture'" (219). Ultimately, however, women and men together put on performances for mixed audiences, ranging from Gogol's "The Wedding" to the prison inmate Karel Schwenk's play *The Last Cyclist*. Often these events, outwardly unpolitical, had underlying political messages. The play *The Last Cyclist*, for example, deals with the only cyclist in a city of pedestrians who is made the scapegoat for all that goes wrong. According to Sedova, this ironic, allegorical play, written especially for Theresienstadt, was based on the "well-known saying that the Jews and the cyclists were to blame for all misfortune" and it caught the attention of the internal self-censorship of the Jewish Council of Elders. The council "wanted to give us permission for the performance only on condition that the ending of the play was struck out." Although the actors agreed, when the play was performed, after the ending, all the actors assembled on stage holding hands and "to the chords of a well-known fighting song ... moved their lips as if they were singing the inciting text" and the audience "knew exactly what was meant" (*Terezin*, Sedova, 224–25). In another essay, another survivor, Arnost Weiss, recounts how an orchestra played the first four bars of the opening of the German national anthem, "Deutschland, Deutschland über Alles" over and over again until "the last outcry 'Deutschland, Deutschland'...did not continue to 'über Alles,' but died out in a terrible dissonance" (*Terezin*, Weiss, 230).

Though each evening entertainment lasted only a few short hours, Sedova says that they gave dignity to the prisoners, and "this spark gave light and warmth for several days" (*Terezin*, Sedova, 224). Spies, who participated in poetry readings, makes the same assertion in her memoirs. She explains that the subjects of the lectures often were remote from daily prison life, but they seemed to have served their purpose, i.e., to make the prisoners forget their dreadful reality for at least as long as the event lasted, and often longer. Perhaps equally important, all cultural activities—plays, musical evenings, poetry readings, as well as the many lectures on various topics—helped to transform "nameless transport numbers into an enthusiastic human community" (*Terezin*, Sedova, 224) and created a spiritual bond between the inmates. Gerty Spies credits these cultural endeavors with helping many of the prisoners survive.

The establishment of a library also played an important role in the life of the prisoners. The library was set up in the Hamburg barracks, and Dr. Emil Utitz, associate professor of philosophy and psychology at Prague University, was in charge of it from 1942 to 1945 (*Terezin*, Starke-Goldschmidt, 172). There was no want of literature, according to

Norbert Fryd, since there was "practically no one who had not brought at least one book in the fifty kilograms allowed him" (*Terezin*, Fryd, 207). Starting with an inventory of 4,000 books, the library contained about 65,000 volumes by May of 1945 (*Terezin*, Starke-Goldschmidt, 175). The books were heavily used, and it is speculated that they, unfortunately, contributed to the spread of skin diseases, jaundice, scarlet fever, and lung and intestinal diseases; this is suggested by the higher-than-average sickness rate among the library staff (*Terezin*, Starke-Goldschmidt, 172). Women like Spies took advantage of the availability of books, even though their state of exhaustion often interfered with their reading.

All prisoners, artists and nonartists alike, shared the daily experience of life and death in Theresienstadt. But as Spies's experience shows, involvement in their artistic activities helped artists as well as amateurs to ignore their surroundings for a while. By no means should these activities be considered peripheral to life in camp; they gave prisoners back their dignity otherwise denied them by their captors. Art became an essential, perhaps the only worthwhile, part of life in Theresienstadt. The artistic struggle helped the prisoners to affirm their own humanity and to keep their spirit alive.

The art of the Holocaust has been regarded as fulfilling a variety of needs. Although the feminist scholar Marlene Heinemann states in her book *Gender and Destiny* that survivors sometimes describe the death camps as beyond language because our languages were never before used to describe such a degree of organized terror (2), a leading function of Holocaust literature was to allow survivors to bear witness and to warn the rest of us about the underside of our civilization. Holocaust literature has also been viewed as contributing to the documentation and interpretation of inhumanity, and as representing a serious appeal to posterity to prevent future recurrences. Another important aspect of this literature was that it provided a psychological survival mechanism. It is this last function which is especially apparent in Spies's writing.

Gerty Spies found her talent amidst the misery of camp life, amidst daily deaths and transports which relentlessly deprived her of newfound friends. She recounts how in a moment of profound despair a redeeming inspiration came to her: "Try writing!... Your thoughts will not again and again grope along this torturous path of suffering, this homesickness. They will have to concentrate—each minute, each second—so that perhaps you can bend your pain into an expression of your imagination.... Only your body will still be here" (Spies, 64). This newfound talent gave her the strength and discipline to transcend her suffering. Here, in isolation from the outside world, surrounded by death, she retreated into her inner self to concentrate on human, religious, cultural, and spiritual values. Her ability to transcend and triumph over mental and physical degradations, to keep her own integrity, to not let evil destroy her loving nature, and finally, to not lose faith in humanity gives Gerty Spies's narrative considerable power. It is the perspective of a sensitive woman and artist who in her youth thought "that the future had only happiness in store for her" (Spies, 31), but who, when faced with evil, found solace in creativity.

"Somebody once said that it is impossible to measure the suffering of an individual. Who then can measure the suffering of so many?" (*Paradise*, Lustig, 12). In his "Some Comments on the Psychology of Life in the Ghetto Terezin," Dr. Jeri Diamant writes that the need for self-preservation caused by the isolation and deprivations of the camp life mobilized prisoners to cope in various ways. Some individuals placed their emphasis on nourishment, others developed asocial traits of behavior, while others retained their cultural interests (*Terezin*, Diamant, 134). Zdenek Lederer in his book about Theresienstadt observed that the "uncertainty of life in the Ghetto…produced a mental climate closely resembling that of puberty" and often found artistic expression in escape poetry (128). Moreover, as Diamant points out, "in the case of some of the more sensitive individuals… there can occur a more permanent retreat into one's own ego …an unreal escape into the past, into reveries, into one's own reflections and thoughts about existence, about the meaning of life, or into mysticism and religion.…Others, especially artists and scientists, tried to break through the barrier of psychic deprivation by holding concerts and lectures" (*Terezin*, Diamant, 130, 135).

The tension that existed between the expression of reality and an idealization of an imagined past is commented on by many scholars of Holocaust art. Reading Gerty Spies's memoirs, one is aware of a curious mixture of naiveté and sophistication, a juxtaposition probably due to psychological scarring from her time spent in Theresienstadt. Idealized pictures of her childhood, retold eighty years later in a tone of

almost forced simplicity, portray her childhood as one picture of innocence if not ignorance. In a similar tone of simplicity, at times bordering on gullibility, she recounts how in
her early attempts to write poetry in Theresienstadt she
sought advice and assistance from "older" men or father figures. Her expressed delight over their responses—they often
treat this woman of forty-six years as if she were a teenager,
a young and innocent child—seem exceedingly naive. Could
Spies really have been unaware that their comments were
patronizing if not condescending? This is the same Gerty
Spies who describes with perceptive insight how she deliber-
ately retreated into herself to overcome the "chronic frustra-
tions" (*Terezin*, Diamant, 135) of irritability and quarrels
brought about by overcrowding and indiscriminately close
proximity to women of different cultural backgrounds and
ethnicity. One of the complexities of Holocaust memoirs is
that the vast majority contain contradictory evidence about
the predominance of selfishness over cooperation in the
camps. Some emphasize such egocentric responses as stealing
food, while others stress the comforting power of conversation, or the pain of seeing others suffer (Heinemann, 81).

Relationships between the different ethnic groups of
Jews, for example, between Czech and Austrian Jews and
between Austrian and German Jews, were by no means har-
monious, as Spies's memoirs confirm. Apparently German
Jews were often not accepted as persecuted Jews but rather
were considered and hated as Germans (Adler, 304). Schwertfeger quotes Hedwig Ems: "The Czechs hated us just as much
as we hated Hitler and they held us responsible for the

calamity that had hit them" (36). Spies alludes gently to some of these tensions, and displays remarkable psychological perception in realizing that her newly found artistic talent would be a support and a force for survival in the face of these emotional strains and physical deprivations. She also credits these artistic activities with helping her regain and secure her sense of individuality, significance, and dignity—an important aspect of survival which the methods and policies of camp administration tried to destroy in all inmates.

With the exception of H. C. Adler's book *Theresienstadt 1941–1945* and Ruth Schwertfeger's book *Women of Theresienstadt*, little has been written about the literary legacy of Theresienstadt. Adler refers to the poetry competitions in which 3,000 poems were submitted from a prison population of 37,000 inmates (615–17). Gerty Spies was one of the poets who entered her works. The certificate of honorable mention which Spies received for her entry is reproduced on page 125 of this work. Adler criticizes the lack of objectivity and the abstract qualities of the poems written during that time. They are, he asserts, nothing but subjective expressions of individual circumstances using more or less naturalistic terms; further, he states, they lack perception, and do not do justice to the seriousness of the situation (616–17). With the exception of two male writers, Georg Kafka and Hans Kolben, Adler rejects the writings of camp poetry as "rhyming sickness" (*Reimkrankheit*, 618). Ilse Weber is the only woman writer of whom he does not entirely disapprove, but even so, he finds her style "irritatingly awkward" (*irritiert unbeholfen*) (619). But as Schwertfeger documents in her book, Adler's judgment can be challenged. Schwert-feger's discussion of different writers together with examples of their work show that some writings are spiritual, some are didactic, and some display a surprising amount of humor, considering the circumstances in which the writers found themselves: some are more abstract than others; some are more naive, simple, and lyrical; some use irony. Almost all of them reveal the writers' awareness of their conditions and a questioning of values. This does not negate the fact that many occasional poems were written, and that even a good portion of lighthearted, humorous works were done for reasons of sheer diversion. Spies comments on this practice and certainly admits to writing her share of these ditties.

However, Spies and other writers also discuss and present definite ideas about poetics, and reveal their struggle for form. Spies describes vividly her struggles in writing poetry, and her profound satisfaction at a well-turned phrase. Of particular relevance here, Spies shows us the transformation of experience into art by including in her book some of the actual pages of her diary written in Theresienstadt. And finally, all writers are in agreement that poetry sustained them, that it helped them deal with solitude and loss. Spies's own survival of her three years in camp, as she never tires of emphasizing in her memoirs and in lectures and interviews, is living proof of the effectiveness of art.

James E. Young, a scholar concerned with writing during and about the Holocaust, points out in *Writing and Rewriting the Holocaust* that "the critical reader accepts that every Holocaust writer has a 'different story' to tell, not because what happened to so many others was intrinsically 'different,' but because HOW victims and survivors have grasped and related their experiences comprises the actual core of 'their story'" (38–39, emphasis/quotes in text). Yet when reading Holocaust literature, we respond not solely to the aesthetics of the survivor's account nor solely to the facts. As Irving Howe puts it, "we respond also to qualities of being, tremors of sensibility, as these emerge even from the bloodiest pages. We respond to the modesty or boastfulness, the candor or evasiveness, the self-effacement or self-promotion of the writers. We respond most of all to a quality that might be called moral poise" (Irving Howe in Berel Lang, 185). I think it is this quality of moral poise which particularly stands out and gives Gerty Spies's memoirs their special significance.

For Gerty Spies, hatred and the desire for vengeance detract from human dignity; blame keeps wounds open; only forgiveness heals. The promise of grace, beauty, and love is worth the struggle for survival. Throughout her memoirs, Spies displays an unwavering belief in the decency, goodness, and sincerity of all people. No trace of cynicism, malice, or misanthropy finds a place in her life or work. Her admonition to "speak to the others, keep on speaking" (*Im Staube,* 75) is expressed in her writings and her acceptance of speaking engagements in order to keep open a dialogue to facilitate understanding between people. Despite living for three years surrounded by horror, Gerty Spies's loving and kind disposition enabled her, as she puts it, "to forgive—but not to forget"; enabled her to return to Munich and reconcile her experiences in Nazi Germany with a new full life as an

artist among newfound friends in Germany after the war—
to return to the country she never stopped considering her
home. Asked why she stayed in Germany, she attributes it to
her love of the language, but "above all, it's the deep friendships which give me strength, which keep me in this country.
It's not letters I want to write. I want to *see* my friends....
Simply for that I would have stayed, although much more
has kept me here" (Spies, 37). Gerty Spies's philosophy of
life is expressed in her often-repeated motto *Verstehen und
Lieben*, to understand and to love.

Spies, the artist, has struggled—I think successfully—to
put into language her individual agony; she can say with
Goethe's Tasso,

> ...and though individuals are silenced by pain,
> a God gave me the gift to express my sufferings.

In translating Spies's book, I have stayed as close to the
original as possible. Memory is selective and the interpretation
of an event depends on the memories associated with it. Writing from "within the whirlwind" (Young, 25), Gerty Spies's
style at times reflects this "association"; she is able to dip into
the future and back into the past at will, when memory serves
her purpose. It takes a skillful artist to bring this off, and an
aware and sensitive reader to follow her. I have not attempted
to make what is difficult to read or understand in German,
uncomplicated or easy in English. Readers need to be alert, and
use their imagination to follow Spies's reflections. No attempt
has been made at rhyming or creating "new" poems in English.

Memory, individual or collective, has always played an important part in Jewish history and culture, helping to keep alive the cultural, religious, and liturgical traditions. Here, in a recollection of the attempted extinction of the Jewish people, individual memory and history are fused to establish the all-important link between the disastrous past and the new and hopeful future. Poetry helped Gerty Spies survive. Reading her story is reading history on a personal level.

Jutta Tragnitz

Works Cited

Adler, Hans Günther. *Theresienstadt 1941–1945. Das Antlitz einer Zwangsgemeinschaft*, 2d ed. Tübingen: Mohr, 1960.

Heinemann, Marlene. *Gender and Destiny: Women Writers and the Holocaust*. Westport: Greenwood Press, 1986.

Lang, Berel, ed. *Writing and the Holocaust*. New York: Holmes, 1988.

Lederer, Zdenek. *Ghetto Theresienstadt*. New York: Fertig, 1983.

Parik, Arnold. "Art in the Terezin Ghetto." In *Seeing through 'paradise,'* edited by Johanna Branson. Boston: College of Art, 1991.

Schwertfeger, Ruth. *Women of Theresienstadt: Voices from a Concentration Camp*. Oxford: Berg, 1989.

Spies, Gerty. *Drei Jahre Theresienstadt*. München: Chr. Kaiser, 1984. Cited as "Spies."

———. *Im Staube gefunden. Gedichte*. München: Chr. Kaiser, 1987. Cited as *"Im Staube."*

My Years in Theresienstadt

Young, James E. *Writing and Rewriting the Holocaust.* Bloomington: Indiana University Press, 1988.
Terezin. Published by the Council of Jewish Communities in the Czech Lands. Prague: 1965. Cited as *"Terezin."*

Preface

This book is composed of personal observations and experiences. In short sketches it tries to convey of what people are capable, whether it be for good or ill, and how the desire for life, love, and beauty can awaken in us an unknown strength. This strength, brought to awareness by suffering, nurtured and sustained by love, directed me in a time of deepest physical and spiritual affliction onto a path where I could do something, could, in my own entirely personal way, shape burning pain as well as devout gratitude into living testimony, could represent myself.

Of course I was afraid; anger and indescribable homesickness tormented me. But again and again my desire to create, my need to capture what I suffered and experienced and what I saw others suffer and experience, took possession of me. I had to write.

This daily conversation with my God drew my gaze away from misery and toward other realities, and bestowed upon me the highest grace a person can be granted—the freedom to be able to forgive.

To forgive—but not to forget: to keep the heart pure from feelings of hate and vengeance. This freedom, this liberation, gave thousands the strength to go with dignity to the most excruciating deaths. May it strengthen us, the living—no matter what our ancestry—and guide us in our striving for mutual understanding.

Gerty Spies

What Is the Guilt of the Guiltless?

What is the guilt of the guiltless—
Where does it start?
It starts there
Where impassively, arms hanging down,
Shrugging his shoulders, he stands aside,
Buttons his coat, lights
A cigarette and says:
There is nothing one can do.
You see, that's where the guilt of the guiltless starts.

"Why Did You Stay?"

To some questions we have no answer, especially if they concern us profoundly. And if one does not have a clear answer, then one must realize that one has not yet begun to find oneself. Now that the question has been posed, one tries to be more aware of oneself: Why is it that you have not yet found yourself?

If now, looking back, I attempt to contemplate and judge and to wrest sense from the long life I've lived with its many different steps, stages, and stops, it seems to me as if I had lived several lives—far away and dreamlike—yet each with its own individual reality. Am I the same one who expected so much from life, who with childlike certainty thought she saw that the future had only happiness in store for her, and who then later, when dreams and hopes blow by blow crumbled under the storms of fate, groped through the darkness seeking God, found paths, began anew—always the same person but each time a different one? And always a new turning point, a new landscape opened up, and the view expanded. Looking back, then, it seems to me as if a hand guided me— even in misery—to new sources, where strength and imagination could flourish, where a new "I" grew out of the old. And yet there are highly individual traits which continue unchanged. They were there from the beginning, they remain, and change perhaps only their color. We carry them with us above all the heights and depths. They were given to us.

Almost every time that I have spoken privately or publicly, as the occasion arose, about my politically determined experiences, there is one voice in my audience (usually a woman) who asks how, after all that I experienced, I could stay in Germany. After all the immeasurable suffering that I experienced and that I had to see, how could I remain in this country, among these individuals, this people, with my many still bleeding spiritual wounds, which will never completely heal. There were relatives over there in the United States, who even after the war would have sponsored me. The authorities would not have made any difficulties either. Why did I stay?

Back then—farther back—when the inconceivable happened and day by day the horror increased in scope, we lived in Munich, on one of the pretty, quiet, tree-lined streets in the northwest neighborhood of Schwabing. Since then I have moved far out to the northern suburbs, where in those days the fragrant forest spread, where pines had their roots under the damp moss and the tender long grass, and where the shallow brooks, quietly trickling, branched out into the darkness. Today there are streets here, and uniform row houses. Everything has changed. Everything?

Only rarely do I find my way through the quiet, elegant street, where nothing concerns me anymore, and where nothing any longer has meaning to me. And I cannot prevent the images from appearing and showing me the way. Such things as happened there! But now I stand before the house in which we lived back then.

Recently, when my granddaughter, who as a five-year-old child had emigrated with her mother to the United States, returned as an adult to spend some weeks in Munich, she wanted to see the house again. She wanted to know whether the sight could awaken memories in her. And she climbed to the fourth floor. But nothing stirred in her; she had forgotten. Not so her mother. The years of persecution had penetrated so destructively into her blossoming youth that she expected to find new strength only in a new, foreign environment. She emigrated—and died in a foreign country of homesickness recognized by no one, and of inner loneliness. Thus I lost my daughter even after the disaster.

We both stood silently on this stairway, my granddaughter and I, she immersed in her thoughts and I in mine. I had to think back to the time of our reunion, when after my three years of exile, my daughter suddenly happened upon me in the street, embraced me, pale and starved as she was. It happened in front of the post office on Leopold Street, under a tree which no longer is there—I believe it was a maple. We could not speak, we could only cry.

My Years in Theresienstadt

Can somebody tell me why I recount all this? I could spill oceans of memories, thoughts, tears, and prayers of gratitude. So long, so full, so sad, so blessed is life. And I started out to explain why I did not emigrate. And even now I still have not emigrated, old as I am, after strange men who listened to me on the radio screamed loathsome obscenities into my phone and left no doubt that the evil spirit is still raging among us. Unemployment and Jew-baiting go hand in hand.

Do persecuted Christian clergymen, socialists, and other courageous fighters also get asked by readers and listeners why they stayed here after the war? Does this question only pertain to Jews?

After I returned to this so miserably destroyed city of Munich, my first outing was to the English Garden. To lie in the grass, to spread out both arms—here I had space!—and to dream up into the treetops! On the large meadow American soldiers played tennis or some other peaceful games—blacks and whites, no racial separation noticeable, at least not there. The blue "rubble flower"—that's what we called it—bloomed throughout the rubble, a delicate veil. And one could sit anywhere—on the grass, on the hills, on the fences and walls. How exasperating that they started to make Munich into an orderly city again! It was so nice, self-evident that everywhere was home and freedom! Nobody paid attention to clothes. Why this troublesome order! We were so uncivilized after the long camp life. And on Feilitzsch Square, which today is called "Munich's Freedom," the little milk house still stood, where they were selling frugal pieces of the much-sought-after leatherlike cake together with thin buttermilk. That was all they had to offer then. Here the poor Polish prisoners had always stood and had waited for their truck to take them to work. You always had a piece of bread or a bread ration stamp in your pocket, because those poor people were starving. Until I was put away ...

And that's what my first days home were like. At first I did not want to see our apartment again, which by pure chance was still standing, although covered with holes from bombs and other damage. But during the course of the year we had to fight hard to keep our own apartment.

But now I was home. At first I celebrated my reunion with the streets, but I avoided some, those whose sight awakened horrible memories in me. Walking was difficult for me. In the small, square camp, after all, we had not been able to walk much further than from the living quarters to work and back again. Now, slowly, my feet were getting used to walking again. And slowly I celebrated my reunion with the mountains. I was able to go and visit all my favorite places again, without anybody restraining me. I visited old acquaintances, if they were still alive. To go long distances I tried using the streetcar. At first it was not running, and later on there were too few of them. One squeezed into it and pressed between the other passengers so as not to fall off. Many had to stand on the steps and hold onto the handles. They were hanging on more than they were standing. We called them "people clusters," which spilled through the doors. There was cursing and quarreling. In fact, there was much quarreling going on and many people complained about hunger "worse than during the war." What could I say to that! My experience had been different.

Life somehow went on wretchedly in a provisional way for everybody. Everything was scarce, from matches to water, which at times had to be carried up from the basement to the attic. And that at night, because during the day no water flowed even in the basement.

Illustrated with some etchings by Otto Nückel, *Theresienstadt,* my book of poetry, was published in 1947 by the publishing house Bruckmann, which had been one of the first to obtain permission to publish from the American occupation government.

The small volume sold unbelievably fast, and now life began to take on new meaning and color. I made contact with a radio station and with many different types of magazines. The *Suddeutsche Zeitung** printed my works. I met all kinds of people, many young ones; I let students live in my home. My mother, who had fled to the United States but never felt at home there, returned to Germany and lived under my care. My life was filled to the brim.

All my Jewish friends had left Germany or had to die. The same had happened to my relatives. Life, especially writing, introduced me to new people, Germans, foreigners, Jews, Christians, and those who felt no tie to any religion. But since I had returned to the land of my language and my homeland, I was able to forge new friendships with its citizens. And although life had taught me to stand on my own

---

**South-German Newspaper*

feet when times demanded it, still I may say that these friendships are my support and my wealth. I love mountains, forests, and lakes. I love the little, pensive towns nestled into the landscape. I love the language, the only one in which I can and could write my poetry. Above all, it's the deep friendships which give me strength, which keep me in this country. It's not letters I want to write. I want to *see* my friends, meet them, love them here in this country, where we speak the same language. Simply for that I would have stayed, although much more has kept me here.

Somebody assured me recently that I had demonstrated courage when I stayed in Germany. Perhaps I am a day-dreamer for whom reality is more an interior place. If, however, courage relies on trust, then the person who told me that is correct. I *do* trust, because—to be brief—I love people with all their faults and weaknesses. Do I love everyone? Do I love them always? At times, daily life produces terrifying lessons. Then I often ask myself: Are other nationalities more mature? I don't know. But I know one thing: Germany is the country of my youth, of my dreams, of my ancestors, of my language. How could I do differently! Germany is my home.

Growing Up in Trier

I grew up in a Jewish family which had been in Germany for many centuries. My parents were Jewish by conviction and at the same time very open-minded—especially my mother, who came from a small town in the Rhineland Palatinate where at that time no discrimination was known. As a young girl, she unknowingly committed a serious faux pas. When a young rabbi was to be elected to her community, in order to recommend him, she happily cried: "Yes, he is a very nice person! He has had dinner at our house—" Here she caught herself—what had she done! That was the end of his being appointed, since my grandmother did not keep a kosher house. The young rabbi should not have eaten at her house.

I was born on January 13, 1897, in Trier, a city of Roman origin, on Brot Street, which was why at age six, when I reported to school, I answered the director's question: "And where were you born?" very accurately, "on Brot Street."

Trier was a garrison town. I accomplished my first extraordinary achievement at about two years of age, when a troop of soldiers marching to music passed our house. I was about to be given a bath, when, being enthralled by the music, I took the opportunity when nobody was watching me for a moment to run out, stark naked as I was, to march in step at the head of the column. Unfortunately, I was interrupted, and I have never tried it again.

When I was four, we moved to Nikolaus Street, where we had a large garden and a stable with a real horse which caught my brother's interest. The animal showed its gratitude one day by biting his hand without any warning, when he tried to feed it.

Old Mrs. Lemmen lived on the fourth floor and we soon became friends. Here I hid out of fear when I was to be painted. Painted! Quite logically, I thought I would be painted the way one paints a wall. My God, how would I look then! However, I was dragged from underneath the bed and was painted after all, and I even became good friends with the painter, whose name was Correggio and who may have been a descendant of his famous namesake. The painting hangs above my head now when I sleep. But that does not bring back my youth.

Another move—this time to Dampfschiff Street, which was so named because Trier was very proud of its newly arrived steamship line and its new ship, on which we were later often allowed to ride. Here I experienced my first serious illness, a bad catarrh of the lungs. And here I also learned for the first time that not all children had as happy a home as we did. We could hear poor Max next door scream pitifully each evening when his father used the rod on him on orders of his stepmother. Poor Max! I don't know what happened to him later in life.

We did not live in this house very long. My father started building the house on Kaiser Street. A little garden graced its façade, while in back there was a larger one which ended at South Avenue.

It may have been 1903 when we moved in. How happy we were that South Avenue was wide enough for all our games. There were no cars yet. Once in a while horses clattered along the asphalt street, or farmers drove their cows to the market. It was quiet and with hardly any traffic. We played skittle, and in the middle of the street we put up the little tower which was to be overturned. We played ball, croquet, and diabolo. My father, who aside from being a business man was also known as a humorous Trier-dialect poet, often took time to play with us during his free evening hours, always undisturbed on the wide street, and sometimes by gesticulating we conversed with the Italian street workers who poured the asphalt and who were almost as playful as we were. When they noticed once that I had to disappear urgently, they generously advised, *"Fa in strada,"** but I preferred not to follow their advice.

Across the street, we climbed over the fence of the

---

*Italian for "Do it in the street"

Roman baths. My brother, one and a half years older and much smarter than I, showed me among the overgrown ruins the subterranean heating pipes which the Romans had used in their era to live comfortably and which also had made it possible for them to take baths, whereas our era no longer knew—or barely yet knew—about such things. Countless wild cats lived in those ruins. At night they prowled the gardens or climbed around on the branches of the nut tree behind the fence. My father usually rented the second floor to officers, whose orderlies, quivering with hunting fever, lay in wait for the poor animals and often killed them. All around us were houses with gardens reaching down to the Mosel River, which flowed gently and pleasantly beneath the old Roman bridge.

During noon hours I often lay in the grass under the acacia trees and dreamily watched the fishing boats until they disappeared behind the bridge. In the evening, we sat under the nut tree listening to the nightingale (what a homely, small gray bird it was!) or sang old folksongs accompanying ourselves on a guitar.

Shortly after our move, I was stricken with the same illness again. My mother had a difficult time with me. I did not want to eat anything. Our doctor prescribed kefir. I hated kefir. He mixed in chocolate chips hoping I would drink it in order to get at the chocolate. I, however, was happy to see the chocolate at the bottom. The only thing that pleased me was oranges. Probably I was responding to a natural craving.

After my recovery I was allowed in good weather to play in the garden, where, among other things, I rescued rain worms. I felt so sorry for the poor things when they came out of the ground after the rain and did not know how to escape the wetness. Carefully, I lifted them up and draped them over the back of the chair, so they could dry out in the sun, the poor things. . . . But it was best to just sit and watch the clouds. Where did they go? And what was behind the mountains? And what was behind what was behind the mountains? And so on—questions and more questions. Once a ladder fell on my head. It did not hurt; I did not notice it at all, but when I was found, I got a lot of sympathy.

In the meantime, I had reached school age. I got used to it quickly; I liked school, even though I soon would find out that little girls often can be very spiteful. On the whole I was satisfied with the women who were my teachers. But nothing is perfect. Next to us lived a pastor with his family. Miss Meyer, the daughter of the pastor, was my class teacher for one year. She did not seem to have a great affection for Jews. One day, something was stolen in class. Without checking into it very thoroughly, she was convinced that I was the thief. When I handed her a letter from my mother the next day, which she read at once, she blushed like a rose. But she was not cured yet. On my way to school, I generally had to pass Wall Street. Usually a schoolmate, whose name was also Gertrud, waited for me there, and she delighted in yelling after me, "Jew, Jew, Jew." When one day she even started it in the schoolyard, I went up to her, took a swing with my left hand (I am left-handed) despite my good upbringing as a girl, and slapped her so hard that she flew against the school-yard wall. The little girls, all about nine years old, instantly flew to Miss Meyer: "Gerty has hit Gertrud!" I explained why. But Miss Meyer said, "For shame! How can you hit a classmate! I am proud if someone tells me I am Protestant. And you hit her. Aren't you ashamed of yourself?" I was shocked, angry, and defenseless. But Miss Meyer did not know my father. Next day he put on his hat—one did not go out without a hat—and visited her. What they discussed I do not know, but things improved from that day on. Subsequently, another pastor and his family moved into the house next to us and we got along with them very well. We children played together and made friends across the garden wall.

There was no religious instruction for Jewish girls in the lower grades. Left to myself I spent my free hours in the halls, and one morning was sitting in the corner under a staircase when the Protestant girls had to change rooms, and passed by me, two by two. "Come with us," they coaxed. "Come along, please do." They were right. Why should I sit around here and be bored? I went with them.

From that day on I learned the story of the little child Jesus, who had come into the world in a stable and who was so sweet and from early on as learned as the wisest men in the temple. It was such a nice story and the teacher was so friendly. I liked learning it. Soon I was one of their best students. One day, when the inspector's visit was imminent, and the best students were selected to take part in a special class in the afternoon, the teacher and the seminar students looked inquiringly at one another. Then they decided to let me come, too. And for me it was a proud event.

But this alliance could not last long. Shortly thereafter, my father received a letter from the senior rabbi asking if he intended to let his daughter become Protestant. With a heavy heart I had to leave. But soon religious instruction started for me as well. It was conducted by the rabbi himself. Dr. Bassfreund liked children, but unfortunately he was not a born pedagogue. Although small in stature, he had a great mind. First and foremost a great scholar, he wrote important books and probably would not have taught had he not had so many children. I was given a Bible now, bound in black, and these beautiful stories appealed to me greatly, too. On my own and because of my delight in the new melodious language, I learned them by heart, one after the other. The rabbi liked that and soon we became friends. And that even though his wife had become very agitated when she discovered a picture of an inadequately robed woman above my parents' bed while visiting my mother during an illness. Well, this was either forgotten or forgiven, and our friendship even went so far that I defended the rabbi. A Catholic priest with the name Cohn who also taught in our school inquired about me, "What is the name of the Jewish girl who does not say hello to me?" At the next opportunity he addressed me, "Why do you not greet me?" I replied: "Because the Catholic children do not greet our teacher of religion." I stood up for justice. This short conversation did not have any consequences, and everything went on as usual. But one day something unexpected happened.

My brother was an extraordinarily talented boy. Drawing and painting were his passion. Without a doubt he wanted to become a painter. One afternoon, unfortunately, religion and drawing were scheduled for the same time. Without thinking, my brother decided: He went to the drawing class. But what happened? During the next religion class, my friend barked at me, "Your brother skipped religion." I explained, "My brother had a drawing class at the same time." He: "That is not true." I: "My brother does not lie." The rabbi became angry; he did not believe me. I defied him. From that time on, I did not answer him when he called on me. Our friendship had turned into irritable tension. Weeks passed. One day, the poor man asked me awkwardly, "Why do you not answer me? What is the matter with you? Don't you like me?" I, in my simplicity: "No." He: "Why?" I: "First of all, my parents think…" "Why did you have to tell this to your parents!" In his ineptitude the poor great scholar had gone too far. My brother and I did not go back to him for instruction.

Years passed. The families broke off all contacts. In 1915, when my brother, a young war volunteer, was in a military hospital with pleurisy, there appeared suddenly in this bare room, which my brother shared with several comrades, a small, bearded man, dressed in black, who walked up to my brother's bed: The rabbi had put behind him all small annoyances. He was the rabbi, and he did what he considered his duty: He visited the sick. My brother was touched deeply and received him gratefully. From that day on the faithful man repeated his visits regularly until the day my brother recovered and was released.

But back to my school days. Each year in September, my two aunts from Cologne and Frankfurt stayed with us in order to visit their parents' graves. It was a wonderful time. They took a horse-drawn carriage from the station to our house, brought presents and stayed a whole week. Festive dinners, family gatherings, love, laughter, merriment. The aunts were pious and prayed every evening by candlelight, for us an unaccustomed, pleasant sight. We still had vacation; the ripe nuts fell from the tree onto the asphalt with a light, dry thump. A wash basket was placed underneath the tree, a man climbed up high into the crown and shook the branches. We harvested, and all the children from the neighborhood harvested with us, ate and filled their pockets. The basket was carried to the storeroom, where we sat down right in the middle of it and only got up after our hands had achieved a uniform black-green color, which took weeks to fade. On days like that we had no room left for dinner.

Now we were heading into autumn, and I was allowed to help my mother take care of the red-cheeked apples from the Mosel region, which are known for their delicious aroma. Each was wrapped separately in newspaper and put one next to the other in baskets, each kind by itself. Our maids in the kitchen had preserved fruit all summer long, singing along—often polyphonically—their favorite songs. I still have the sound of one of them in my ears:

> No, no, no, no, it is not here,
> The home of the soul is above in the light.

Their fiancés, they called "treasure"—whom they later really married—sat with them, ate with them, and helped fix things or pitched in when something needed to be done around the house. Thus we very seldom needed workmen. Sometimes I

47

joined this merry group, had them tell me tales, or told tales myself, sang with them, and often little troubles disappeared in these surroundings.

Generally we spent the evenings around the family table. Friends came. It was a home full of warmth and sociability. But nights often lay heavy on my heart. After it was dark and quiet, and when nothing moved any longer, I listened to the creaking of the parquet floor, which could be heard over and over again. My heart beat violently. Oh my God, that had to be a thief who had crept in, or perhaps even a murderer! For minutes I stopped breathing so he would not hear me. If only he would not find my parents. Often it lasted for hours, until I finally fell asleep. But my thoughts about the future were even worse. I knew that one day one of us four would have to die first. Who? And how to go on living when one was missing? Impossible! And so I lay awake and often cried bitterly, alone with my anxiety, spoke to nobody about it, and kept this worry all to myself in my timid child's heart.

At Christmas time, my grandmother came with a suitcase full of home-baked goods. Right away she put a full bowl in front of us and let us eat to our heart's content. Often, Uncle Löwe came too, who played with us so well and had the most eccentric ideas. Once he set his feather bed on fire, because he wanted to smoke in bed. Another time, we were all sitting comfortably around the table when suddenly he jumped up, yelling, because a box of matches had abruptly caught fire in his pants pocket. What startling things smoking can cause. He was altogether a fiery man. As an old man, many years later, he perished miserably in Theresienstadt.

My way to school was through the center of town. In those days one could ride the horse-drawn streetcar. But why spend money for something unnecessary! A half-hour walk to school is healthy. Later came the electric streetcars, about the same time that students from the gymnasium started wearing colored caps, depending on which grade they were in. The first streetcar was an earthshaking event when it went through Fleisch Street, decorated with its little flags. That day turned into a festival. But as I said, we took the streetcar only in emergencies. Each ride was ten pfennigs. My brother and I left the house together every morning at the same time. Since he turned off at Böhmer Street, while I had to cross the main market square, trekking down Glocken Street, I was late almost every day. Not to mention that the route I took was full of beauty. To the left and right the witnesses of bygone centuries surrounded me, from the earliest Middle Ages to the Bismarck era; finally the panorama was completed with the view of the Porta Nigra, the ancient Roman city gate. Anyone growing up in a city like that has a difficult time coming to terms with the spectacle of concrete blocks going up by the hundreds nowadays. Even our school had originally been an early Baroque monastery, next to a small Baroque church. In our free time, we climbed up high into the mysterious, gloomy rafters. Two of my classmates made it to the attic of the church, where once they even pulled on the eternal lamp from up above. Whoever sat down below just then praying perhaps experienced a peculiar fright and may now believe in ghosts or miracles.

To be reached within a few minutes, and dominating all its surroundings, was the cathedral. The way to it was through two alleys. One was called "Cattle dance" and the other "Look about you." This warning was addressed to all those miscreants and exiled people who within the cathedral's vicinity—within the cathedral's immunity—were protected from arrest. Should they, however, step into these alleys, the protection ended, and they needed to look around carefully to see if they had been discovered and were now being pursued.

Once on the way home through one of these alleys, walking four abreast taking over the whole width of the street—I, my girlfriend, my brother, and his friend—we met our English teacher. We curtsied, as we had learned, and the boys bowed and raised their caps. Next day, blushing with embarrassment, Miss Jäger pulled me aside: "Gertrud, who were those two young men?" The poor woman felt a responsibility to watch over my virtue. She breathed a sigh of relief when she learned that it had been my brother under whose protection we had walked. That I could be lying to her never even entered her mind.

I was a rather dreamy creature. One day, when I was crossing the main market square, the market women watched me strangely, shaking their heads. What was the matter with me? I could not discover anything extraordinary. Arriving at school I took off my coat, and reaching to my head, I was paralyzed with dismay: I had forgotten my hat, had walked to school without a covering for my head! I was deeply ashamed, I was laughed at and mocked. My God, without a hat! Luckily, my mother discovered what I had forgotten in time and sent one of our maids to school to hand this indispensable item to me furtively during the break.

We were grown now. My brother, Rudi, belonged to the group "*Wandervögel*" who often came to the house, singing and accompanying themselves on the guitar. When they went hiking, they were in front of our gate early in the morning sounding their peculiar whistle. The blackbird quickly learned their five-tone melody and started imitating them. Sometimes they took me with them on their outings. Once, when my girlfriend also went with us on one of these, she had to endure a terrible scolding. Her father, a rector, was incensed that his daughter had dared to go for a walk in the woods with young men without supervision of older persons. This old-fashioned man was nonetheless a splendid human being.

He had heard me recite poetry several times at the birthday celebration for the emperor, was enraptured, and when planning a social evening suggested to his academic colleagues that I be asked to recite poetry. They declined. Why? Because I was Jewish. The old gentleman got so excited that he suffered a heart attack. He died soon afterwards. His daughter, then my girlfriend, is said to have turned into a fanatical National Socialist.* I lost all contact.

As we know, not everything was good and serene in "the good old days." There was much poverty, and the difference between rich and poor was much greater than nowadays. Only when I was older and took up a career in social work did I come into contact with these kinds of problems.

---

*Nazi

51

And now just a few more words about relatives and about the merry carnival times in the Rhineland. Uncle Julius and Aunt Olga had two sons, but no daughter. This explains—and I found it very agreeable—why they chose me as the object of their indulgence. Often when I passed their store and Uncle Julius saw me, he quickly grabbed me by the arm and took me to Amlinger, a café next door, to buy me cake or "Quittenwürstchen." Since my brother and I confided in each other, he was very well informed about this tradition and practice. Toward the last days of carnival, my father had the mezzanine of his store emptied out as much as possible, so that we could invite our friends to a dance. Once, on Monday before Lent, my mother and I came disguised as dominoes.

Brother Rudi, however, came disguised as "Gerty." Uncle Julius was not quite sure of himself: Was this really Gerty? Or was it someone else? Maybe even a male creature? Aunt Olga was summoned. She put up her lorgnette and examined the capering creature from all sides. Finally she concluded: "Yes, that's her. You can tell by her legs," she pronounced in her Frankfurt dialect. The sweet creature now grabbed Uncle Julius's arm, flattered him, and caressed his cheeks. How he loved to take her to Amlinger! They were both very happy and stayed there almost half an hour. When they returned, Rudi held a large bag in his hand. But when he suddenly lifted his mask, my good uncle was speechless. He could only stammer, "How, how, what?" Then he fell into a chair to laugh with the laughers. And everything dissolved into a joyful dance. Then we moved into the street in a long colorful line, my brother at the head with his accordion. There we continued to dance.

On a day like that I was kissed on the hand for the first time in my life. The young freshman—shy and awkward as I—a friend of my brother's, died of TB after the war. My brother died shortly before the end of the war, on September 15, 1918, as a lieutenant of the Reserve at the western front. He was the first of the four of us who had to leave. Twenty-three years we were allowed to have him with us, to love him, to live with him. A reason for deep gratitude. Many years later we still heard the blackbird imitate the whistle of the "*Wandervögel*." It, too, had not forgotten.

I never went back to Trier after my mother moved away from there in 1929, two years after my father's death. I want to let these memories live on within me undisturbed.

That's How It Was

Early, when on your way to work
You measure the black-holed street,
The corners whisper to you:
Don't forget, you are a Jew.

And if you search, to devour your bread,
For a bench in a quiet place,
The bench screams: Get up, you Jew!
You bolt up terrified and sneak away.

When children during their play
Turn after the shadow of your shadow,
You can see in their bright features
Nothing but the grinning of the devil.

When a sharp look lightninglike
Hits you from the side and recognizes you—
The pavement arches toward you,
Your heart freezes, your soles burn.

If in the tired evening hours
The doorbell's piercing sound hits your ear,
The chair shoots you out of its arms:
Now they are here. Now they will take you.

You seek the forest. The trees murmur,
And "Jew" they murmur without cease.
The echo swells, the mountains call
to you "Jew, Jew, Jew!"

It chases you across bare fields,
Through quiet villages you flee.
Alone! Alone!—There it screams from inside:
Oh curse, that I am a Jew.

You cling to the dead stones
Tightly and you listen to them,
Whether they will not come to life
And shout your guiltless disgrace.

What matters hunger's raving gnawing,
The streaming army of homeless ones!
Whoever has experienced such torments,
His heart has broken and it will never heal again.

How I Survived It

The seventeenth of July 1942 was a warm summer day. I went home from an evening visit—furtively, anxiously, looking all around me to see whether I was observed. For it was long past nine and I should not have been out anymore. Stop, no light in the hallway—better to fumble upstairs in the dark. The house was full of treachery, full of foreign eyes.

I opened the door, turned on the light. A thick yellow letter was on the floor. What was that? My heart started to beat violently. From the Jewish Cultural Society? I ran into the room, put the letter on the table—I knew everything: The transport.

It was very quiet in the apartment; my daughter had gone out. With shaking hands I opened it; I read an immense number of regulations, commands—everything went blank before my eyes; I started to run back and forth in the large apartment, the speechless rooms—no sound, no human soul! What to do? How to deal with this monster which had attacked me? Had they not assured us again and again that the so-called prominent people would not be put away?

In my confusion I ran out. What else could happen if I disobeyed this order! To be alone was worse.

The people on the first floor were always friendly. They still said hello, even now. Surely they would let me make a telephone call. My own phone had already been taken away.

I rang the bell. I rang it again. Oh yes—it was already after ten. A disturbance in the night. But now I heard footsteps. Thank God. The man of the house opened. "Excuse me," I said, "I beg you to allow me to make a telephone call." He looked at me; he did not say a word—perhaps he thought I was ill-mannered? I had to explain, to win his heart. With great reluctance: "I—I will be taken away—with the transport—I—"

Here the man shook his head, looked at me sadly, and closed his door. I ran outside.

Here, everything was darkened. It was war, after all, and the city was covered in total darkness. It started to rain. I spoke to a stranger, asking him to give me a light in a telephone booth. He wanted to know why. I told him. He was alarmed, gave me some light, and fled. From my fate? From his conscience? I called an acquaintance, could he spend the night at my house—please! The rain grew heavier, I waited. An hour later we arrived at home, totally drenched.

Shortly thereafter my daughter came home. I turned off the light. Let her think I had gone to bed already. Let her sleep one more night quietly and without care.

Three days later she stood by the window and looked down the street when the big black car arrived. She turned to me; her face was as white as the wall. "They are coming," she said. And then came the farewell.

From Camp Milbertshofen, where they kept us overnight and where they lightened our luggage by half its weight, a closed furniture truck took us to the train. On a side track, we were loaded onto the train. From the surrounding homes binoculars were turned on us. The train left. Who of us would ever see Munich again?

And now: Were we going to Poland? Or to Czechoslovakia? The men watched station by station. Theresienstadt, they had told us, was a camp for the privileged. Perhaps it was "only" Theresienstadt we would have to endure? We were an oddly thrown together community, as we sat there, all strangers and yet bound together by the darkness of the future, the fear, and—at this hour—by the threat of being shot, should we put our heads out of the window.

The next day we arrived in Bauschowitz, Czechoslovakia. Light rain falling from low-hanging clouds. In the mud and the rain, old and sick people were lying about, left there from the transport which had arrived ahead of us from who knows where, and waited to be called. We went on foot to Theresienstadt. Our luggage was to follow.

First sight upon our arrival: A funeral car not drawn by horses. People pulled it. Also, no coffins—bread was transported in it. An entire funeral car filled with loaves of bread for the banished. Later, we got used to this sight.

After they looted our hand luggage, we were led through

the village. Incredible! Where was the senior citizens home, the residence of which they had spoken to us? Where were the clean houses, where everybody would have their own well-furnished room? Through open doors we saw shapes in rags lying on the floor or on wooden frames. Groups of misery were led to pick up food; each carried his own little container in his hand.

They took us to our quarters.

But we could not live here! It was a shed in the back of a courtyard. In this yard, an ugly-smelling compost heap—high as a hill—stewed in the burning midday sun. There was nothing in the shed. No furniture, no oven, no stove—only the floor, the roof, and rags hanging from the walls. Here our existence in camp began.

On the first evening, as we were standing around in the empty shed, wondering whether there wasn't another possibility than lying down on the bare floor, apparitions of hunger came to us out of their cavelike doorways. They approached step-by-step and finally they stood before us. "I have not heard for a long time—what's happening in the world. Don't you have a newspaper?" But then came the truth—they begged for bread. We gave these apparitions of hunger whatever we still had. Poor, poor people, we thought —and nothing else. We did not think further: Soon we will be such poor, poor people, too.

The next day we got bread for three days. Two days later we had to throw it away. It was moldy.

Old Neumeier was the first to die. Actually, he had arrived with us almost dead. Someone else followed him, a man in his best years. He had been so vigorous and cheerful, had supervised the distribution of bread with much authority, humor, and experience. He died because he did not get the medicine on which he depended to stay alive. The dying went on.

In the old house, built around the courtyard, with arcades, outside stairways, rooftop terraces, uncounted corners and crannies, there lived around five hundred people. Each person was allotted a living space about two feet wide. The length of the space was enough to sleep with bent knees. For this large community there were two toilets in the house. And we all had diarrhea—hunger does that to you quickly. It was not very long before our eyes were inflamed. The dust of the unpaved streets was filled with germs which also attacked the respiratory tract. Other illnesses were rampant: Typhus, TB, erysipelas, phlegm—two from our transport volunteered as nurses. In each house there was a so-called sick bay.

We got used to it, learned to get our food in the army courtyard, learned to eat it slowly, with deliberation, spoonful by spoonful, so as to value each gram; learned to get along with one another; we, who were so different, learned to support each other, learned to accept that they had even stolen our last bit of luggage—in short, we learned to accept poverty, the limited space, the imprisonment, the not being oneself any longer, learned to recognize death as a common acquaintance. But our thoughts were hidden deeply in our innermost selves. There, something lived that was holy, pure —the dream of another planet. The other planet was home.

At night, when the others slept, when noise and arguments had quieted down, then I became conscious of our accursed fate in its entire gravity. There I lay on the bare, hard floor and imagined how things were going at home, how such a young girl now could manage her life alone, the loneliness, the cruelty of her surroundings. From crying I went to praying and finally to sleep.

We were commandeered to work. I reported for mica-slate work. It was a workshop within a large barrack, where mica-slate was split very fine, until it was like paper and flexible. We sat in groups of twelve at long tables, bent over the work all day long, and gave it all the strength we had. The summer was unbelievably hot, the barrack hot and sweltering. The women talked about home.

What was this splitting of the mica-slate good for? I found that out only after a while.

In August 1942, on the instructions of a firm from Tabor (South Bohemia) a place to split mica-slate was opened up in Theresienstadt. For a long time this workshop was located in one long barrack within the camp and it was only later enlarged and relocated into two larger barracks outside of the fortress in the so-called cauldron of Bauschowitz.

The mica-slate was delivered in large blocks and then broken up into small, flat membranes, the so-called coarse splinter process. Then it was brought to our barrack for the so-called fine-splinter process where the mica membranes were split again and again into paper-thin, flexible, small sheets with knives in the form of flat letter openers which were developed specially for this process—until they could not be split any longer. Since mica-slate can absorb a high degree of heat without burning, it was used to insulate electrical instruments; in fact, it was used especially in the airplane industry, and therefore our workshop was considered important to the war industry.

In September 1944, piecework was introduced. The women workers were seated according to output, and the demands steadily increased. Whoever did not fulfill their quota was in danger of falling victim to the next transport. Many women died this way. By the end of the war the possibility for its use in industry declined more and more. From spring 1945 on it was only a sham production, and yet we had to continue to do piecework until Theresienstadt was liberated by the Russians and the production stopped.

Oh, these women and their never-ending chatter! While their fingers worked the mica-slates, they spoke of their families, of their camp experiences, about food, and about work. And I sat there and could not be part of their conversation.

I never felt as lonely as I did among all these people. With tenacious force my thoughts drew me back. Homesickness and worry did not leave space for other thoughts. My hands became slower; because of tears I could not see the mica-slate any longer.

Today I find it impossible to retrace the chain of images and thoughts which my will to survive then knew how to forge from my inner reserves. All was resistance and despair within me, and often I was so overcome that the work fell out of my hands. With obstinate defiance I looked at my boss, this good person, a prisoner himself, who was responsible to the Gestapo for whatever happened in the mica workshop. Could even he not help?

Suddenly he stood next to me, spoke to me, tried to comfort me. But my tears kept coming. It was useless. Then he sent me outside. For five minutes I was alone with myself. I stood outside, leaning against a tree. I often think about this tree. The guard, a young person, came down from the rampart and wanted to know why I was crying so hard. I told him I was homesick and just once did I want to go up on the rampart and look across the countryside, at the street going west. But, as sorry as he was for me, he was not allowed to let me go up. He, too, tried to comfort me—it all will pass, and one day.... Did he himself live to see that day?

The weeks passed. Reluctantly I did my dull work, all the time brooding unceasingly over my cares and thoughts. Until suddenly, out of deepest despair, the redeeming idea blossomed, shyly and only weakly delineated at first: Try writing. Your father, your ancestors, all have done some writing; even you yourself have attempted it at times. What could happen? Your thoughts will not again and again grope along this torturous path of suffering, this homesickness. They will have to concentrate—each minute, each second—so that perhaps you can bend your pain into an expression of your imagination. You will not hear any longer what happens and what is talked about around you. Only your body will still be here.

I did not have grandiose plans. It was to be a few simple children's songs. I would go on from there. I did not know then that the protecting angel whom I had selected was to lead me, consoling me, through three years of my life.

And so I started.

My first attempt was a poem for children:

The Clock

Tick tock, tick tock, on the wall,
Listen to me go.
But if your hand forgets me,
I stand still.

My honest face
You may trust.
Only I do not like you to
Look into my heart.

Night comes in a dark dress,
Listen to me strike:
Dear child, it's time for sleeping,
Let me tell you.

All is resting, only I alone
May not stop.
Sleep in God's arms,
Let him rule.

It was difficult to conjure paper for my writing from the nothingness of our misery, but necessity finds a way. I knew how to obtain a small red notebook, but its capacity was soon exhausted. What now?

In November when the cold weather started and our workshops were furnished with stoves, I volunteered as stoker. Diversion, movement, exertion up to deathlike exhaustion—this was the other medicine I prescribed for myself. Those who during working hours—because of rushing and struggling—did not have time for reflection, and who fell asleep from exertion during free time, were better off—even if it meant losing their health. Of what value is health, when the main concern must be to overcome the devilish torture of the soul—homesickness, imprisonment, worry, disgust, and inner loneliness!

And this remedy helped—and without weakening the healing power of the first. I returned from work to my living hole—and fell asleep immediately. I got up between three and four o'clock in the morning, slid over the icy courtyard to get water in the dark and under enormous difficulties, to clean my tiny sleeping place. By five o'clock in the morning, I would already be in the mica workshop removing sediment from the ovens using a hammer and searing cold poker—and creating a poem while doing it.

As a Stoker Woman

*One woman saws and chops the wood
And splits it into pieces.
The other withdraws, quiet and proud
From the day's noise.*

*One woman feeds the stoves,
Cleans away both cinder and soot;
She hammers coal into smaller pieces
And subdues the embers and flames.*

*The other woman, in search of the spirit,
Breaks through invisible barriers.
She dreams and listens to nature,
Creates songs out of thoughts.*

*From time to time the two
Embrace each other with bright laughter.
Out of their kiss my being ascends,
A child of dreaming and waking.*

Whoever has to make a fire needs paper, and whoever needs paper gets permission to enter the packing room. There stood a roll of packing paper, high as a man, to be used for packing the mica slate. I had found my solution: from now on, I wrote my poems on packing paper.

It was harder getting wood. To be sure, there had to be heat. Nobody could work with fingers stiff from cold. But wood was not distributed and it was forbidden, under considerable penalty, to look outside for branches, boards, or beams lying around. I had to figure out what to do—in short, I had to make a fire, but without wood.

It meant getting up even earlier, to be in the barracks already at 4 A.M. There was a pit close to the mica workshop where a latrine had been torn down. The fragments were lying now under a crust of snow and ice. I crept there in the early morning darkness. I knelt down, and with both hands started to dig out of the crusted snow the huge beams, which were almost as long as a barrack was wide. How I managed this feat, I can't fathom any longer. It was heavy work for men—and I did it at my own risk and, so to speak, always looking over my shoulder in constant fear of being discovered and reported to the SS, to become a victim of my courage. Once it finally was dug out of the ice, this beam—of which all the women were afraid because they swore that as a consequence of its past, it carried all the germs and epidemics of Theresienstadt within it—this beam needed to be dragged back to the barrack undetected. And it was so long that I had the greatest difficulty towing it into the barrack. If it stayed dark, it would be all right, but if a window were to light up opposite in the Magdeburg barrack, the light would throw a wide, golden beam across the snow, and I saw my shadow, large and treacherous, moving across the barrack wall, and the never-ending shadow of the beam staggering in front and in back with me. My heart pounded, the sweat of fear dripped out of my pores. And once I was caught. But luckily, it was only someone from the ghetto guards, thus himself a Jew. He should have denounced me—we had a long deliberation—but at his own risk he let it go with a warning. And I kept on "towing" the forbidden, indispensable, necessary wood.

Now I had reached the door. But how to get it in? Here my old friend Falkenstein helped me. He had arrived with a transport from Frankfurt and was actually a butcher by trade. But in Theresienstadt he did not want to remember this any longer. I could not expect anybody to help me with the "towing." But once at the door, there was less danger. The old man gave me a hand, helped me turn it and carry it; he put one end on a low wooden box, and with his legs swollen from hunger, he sat down astride the beam and started hitting it with an ax, so that the splinters flew all over. "Only for you," he used to say, when he was too tired to even lift his arm. He had taken such a liking to me, because I had to do this forbidden work, which nobody even dared to order me to do. Later, he had to stop; he, too, perished from privations in Theresienstadt.

The cold weather did not let up; we lacked clothing, underwear. We had a "Camp Welfare Office" which was overwhelmed with petitions. How could I make them aware of me and my unbearable poverty? I had an idea: a poem! A humorous poem.

What was needed was a little inner jolt: I had to set myself apart from the gray masses of the people at large. With pounding heart, I begged my boss for a piece of white paper; after all, I could not send a petition on packing paper, that would not do. He assented gladly, but I could not prevent his being interested in the writing which his stoker, after some reflection, put on paper.

I had won his heart. His heart and his interest. "Leave your poem with me. I will give it to my brother-in-law who works in the Welfare Office." With a smile he folded the white sheet and put it in his pocket.

So what had I done? A humorous occasional poem—nothing unusual. The manager of the Welfare Office—it, like everything else, was subordinated to the camp self-government (even though the whole camp was under constant pressure from above and only governed with a pretense of ghost-like, mechanical freedom)—this manager of the Welfare Office asked to see me. I stood facing him and was surprised. So, my poem was different from the many hundreds of poems which he had run across? Strange—why exactly mine?

Something good came from this. He granted my modest requests as far as the wretched conditions of the camp allowed, and my boss allowed me to write. If my four stoves were going, if wood and coal had been procured and cut into pieces, if the tiny portions for our midday meal had been consumed by the workers—a task I had to supervise—then he passed me smilingly and turned a blind eye when he saw me sit on my wooden crate and write.

Winter covered the world of our barracks with its white linen cloth. Hunger, homesickness, weakness kept me strained and paralyzed. But a day was a long time, and during this long time there always was some moment in which to let my thoughts fly, like birds hungry for air, and to lead the pencil unobserved across the unruly paper, where words obeyed almost effortlessly, so that my innermost self sang with jubilation, with joy and astonishment.

Thus I was somewhat armed spiritually when in the spring of 1943 a severe case of pneumonia seized me and flung me onto my dirty sack of paper where I languished for several weeks in a damp hole of a basement. The fever was not sure whether to burn me up or to let me go again. But my nature knew all the more what it wanted. Whereas my doctor, Dr. Ruben, tried every way and did not spare himself to save me—not suspecting that soon after he would be sent to his own death—my thoughts, in wise premonition, searched for secluded paths in my imagination where no pain can hurt, no fire can burn any longer. And so my feverish dreams removed me from the danger which surrounded me, made me insensible to it by allowing me to live totally within myself, or—if I may so describe it—to transcend it all.

Unforgettable is the day when Dr. Ruben, with a sigh of relief, let go of my pulse and nodded contentedly. I fell back on my cot and closed my eyes, and to my inner gaze there opened up a cluster of dark clouds through which, from a boundless, immeasurably deep heavenly distance—like an emblem of supernatural grace—pierced a bright beam of light. This blinding light of grace from another world pronounced: You have been saved.

Everybody will understand that this experience filled me with deepest gratitude, and that this gratitude generated a new creative impulse in me. The following summer, despite all its sufferings and privations of imprisonment, brought forth one of the greatest, most beautiful miracles of my life: Out of the dark soil of my sorrows there sprang forth creatures of my imagination, pictures of memories, like radiant blossoms. Everything that I was deprived of, my home, beauty, liberty, love, enjoyments of the past, they all were granted me anew. Today, my hometown on the river with its towers, gray from age; tomorrow, the mountains, lakes, and forests—everything that life had jumbled up within me took on color and urgently sought outward form.

The nights did not let me sleep and, while the regular breathing of my companions filled the cramped room with a muffled heaviness, I lay awake, tossing back and forth, forming images with feverish delight and anguish until the images which invaded me had been transformed into language. Only with the early morning prayer of the blackbird did I fall into liberating sleep, often crying with gratitude. I had done my work.

Yet despite all that, it was not a free or easy sleep. I could not and was not allowed to turn on the light during the night. My poetic creations often were long and therefore difficult to retain in my memory. Then I started the habit (today I cannot fathom how in my physical weakness I summoned the tenacity) with unrelenting energy, while forming and shaping word for word and line for line, to chisel them into my memory, always repeating them again anew in my mind, going on a little, and then repeating all of it over again, and so forth. And all that without letting slip away my underlying mood necessary for creating. I held on to them, they held on to me—together we held each other, my creatures and I. The sober morning tore me out of my half-sleep with noise and light, and still staggering and not in possession of my senses, I started to drum into myself the creations of the night again, while my hands were groping for the washbowl and my feet carried me to the sink. Even then I still did not find the time to write it all down. Often it was noon, indeed, sometimes evening before I got to it.

With all his kindness and goodness of heart, my doctor was a boisterous ball of fire—we loved him even more because of it. He was the first who taught me a lesson. I had warmed his heart with a poem of gratitude, arousing his admiration with a humorous creation in which the various species of molesting vermin appear in a triumphal parade. Here is the beginning:

> *Gnat, bug, louse and flea,*
> *Hah, what a life!*
> *Of course humans are not so gay.*
> *No matter. In bed and straw*
> *It crawls, wheezes, and leaps about.*
> *Can there be anything nicer?*

And so on.

One day by chance one of my lyrics fell into his hands, and as I felt a blush wash over my face as though I were a young girl, I accepted his advice: "Very good, very good. But not quite mature. *Dichten*, writing poetry," and his hands moved toward each other, as if he squeezed the air between them, forming and rounding it, "*dichten*, to be sure, does not come from *dicht*, 'dense'—although many people think so. But think as if it were so. More terse, charged with meaning, more concentrated. It is between the words, between the words."*

For the beginner, every critique is a mountain, for, understandably, she begins to doubt herself. Nothing had as yet proven to her that there could be an external reason to represent her own experience creatively.

From the kind of reaction I had, I easily saw that I was not just interested in distracting my troubled thoughts. And it was not a question of success, but rather it was the obstinate, tenacious striving to do what I did fully, to demand even from a hobby—anxiously groping—my very best that lay within the limits of my talent. From now on, I retreated even more into myself.

My pleurisy caused a weakened heart condition which freed me from forced labor for a while. At this time, the bulwark was made available to us. It meant, until rescinded, permission to go there during certain hours outside of working time. Up there it was possible to be alone with oneself. Though two feet away another person also seeking solitude might lie on his back, dreaming into the sky, one felt unobserved. It was quiet, the sun warmed one with love, and the view which offered itself to the eye could transport even the most sober mind away from reality.

Far in the distance, the rounded shapes of the Bohemian foothills were fading into the silver blue sky. The castles

---

*An untranslatable pun in German, from *dichten*, "composing or writing poetry," and *dicht*, "dense" or "tight"

which towered with a bold gesture into the sunset seemed so unreal in their antiquated beauty that one always had to ask oneself anew—especially after a year of imprisonment: Did your wishful dream magically put them there, or did the hand of history years ago assign them this throne from which they so venerably look out over lands and forests?

Toward evening, the wind often collected itself from all directions and, as if it knew of our misery and wanted to comfort us with a brilliant display of colors from the setting sun, it drove the evening array of clouds into herds, waves, veils, fleeing birds, and sailing ships, which often filled the entire sky with their performance, from a faint iridescence of turquoise to a dark glowing purple, satiating the eyes so lavishly that in our torment-filled nights the colors came alive anew underneath our lids: "Don't forget to be grateful!"

Up there, on the sandy gray waves of the hill of the bulwark a few short poems came to life. I was lying there, breathing and drinking in the sun—living a little. I took the lifesaving mood of these hours with me into my nights. Hungry and homesick, I still had space in my innermost self for this woeful bliss, and I walked between the humpbacked houses on the uneven pavement—yet I was not there. Daily transports came and went, thousands of feet whirled the disaster-steeped dust into our lungs; we had one infection after another. Life—close quarters, vermin, hunger, constraint, and fear—everything was terrifying, existence unbearable, the body weak, nerves shattered, continued existence impossible.

And I wrote.

With our transport had come an old lady, Eugenie Gorter,

who watched over me like a mother. I could not stop her when one day without a word, she took some of my strips of packing paper and withdrew into a corner to read. That was a decisive hour. They had even sent blind people to Theresienstadt. Even highly cultured minds whom the fatherland should have thanked for valuable inventions and creations came together, finally got to know one another in a sad fulfillment of long-cherished desires and sweetened somewhat for one another the bitterness of this existence.

Combining both in herself—being blind and being entitled to the gratitude of a nation by virtue of a life of creativity—an elderly lady, the German poet Elsa Bernstein, who had published her works under the pseudonym Ernst Rosmer, subsisted, starved, froze, and lived on the abundance of her spiritual richness.* Elsa Bernstein lived together with Eugenie Gorter. I owe to Eugenie's intercession the encounter, so valuable for me, with this great woman. At another place in this book I have tried to put into words how much I owe to "Mrs. Elsa," as we called her, for her instructions and power of imagination, her encouragement and my growing self-confidence.

It turned fall again. Outside the rampart birch trees stood in flames. My hands took up again the work of heating; they had to dig the coal, piece by piece, with naked fingers out of

---

*Elsa Bernstein, née Porges, was a granddaughter of Franz Liszt, and mother-in-law to Gerhard Hauptmann's son Klaus-Ernst Rosmer (Adler, 817).

the bins—since no shovels were available—to feed the fire. Again I walked around in my long work pants, and my thoughts sought their own paths. If until then it had been memories of home, the past, which formed themselves out of me into a life of their own, now Theresienstadt itself, with the apparitions of its darkness, began to press for liberation. Only now did I start to shape Theresienstadt: the first distancing had been won. Now my inner self hurled out of itself all that had accumulated. I became a volcano—and found relief.

Thus arose the poems of hunger, of misery, and of suffering, which mirrored the hell of our existence. Astonished by the deep impression they called forth, I realized that they expressed what others also felt, and that they left an enduring echo in their minds.

Here I want to recall the many artistic performances, which alone would suffice—even if nothing else had happened in Theresienstadt—to erect a lasting memorial to the history of Jewish culture. What enormous strength was required to raise oneself up and to gather from the stars what the earth denied. There were innumerable performances, all under a combined administration, the so-called free time activities. It started during the summer of 1942 with lectures by Professors Stein, Jakobsohn, and Münzer (who used to gather his audience about him in a backyard. He died later that same autumn, a victim of Theresienstadt).

In this first summer I experienced a concert in the attic of the Dresdner barracks. Some women sang with beautiful trained voices—and hungry stomachs—and carried us off for an hour into the world of oblivion. I can't remember their names, yet I am grateful to them still today. How richly rewarded one left such performances is difficult to describe. Even more exalting than our artistic pleasure, often diminished by the circumstances, was the effect of the triumph on our spirits: Strike away—you cannot conquer us! Stephan Zweig's immortal words: "You can conquer a people, but not its spirit!" became more vivid for me than ever before.

Gratefully I would like to recall an old gentleman whom fate had torn from his circle of activity in Berlin: Philipp Manes. He had been a furrier and had traveled widely. Arriving on one of the first transports from Berlin, he and several companions had been given the office of "orientation service" in the Magdeburg barracks. They were to assist the people arriving with transports by day and by night with accommodations, and help them in getting used to camp. To fill the intervals of waiting and watching, these men, at his suggestion, sat in a circle and started telling each other about their lives. Philipp Manes recognized early that only mental turning away from the misery of the crushing present made it possible to survive this time of trial with dignity. Under his guidance, these tales became reports, the reports became performances, and thus, quietly, a significant cultural organization originated here, amidst gloomy barrack walls, lacking light day and night, surrounded by garbage, misery, epidemics, and death.

In this setting the Czech writer and translator Aurednicek held her fascinating lectures. Anybody who heard her even only once will never forget her. She had experienced great suffering, and she mustered heroic strength to ignite her spirit for two poor but rich hours of oblivion—and recount to her spellbound audience her literary remembrances from works of Czech writers and about her encounters with them. She stood up there on the shaky podium, her beautiful white hair in a knot, a wide scarf around her shoulders, her eyes like two fiery fountains, and her warm voice drew everything from her memory that could radiate joy and courage.

Here, at Manes's gatherings, the psychology professor Emil Utitz also gave several of his scientific lectures. Dialogues which were to help protect us against the physical and moral assaults of camp life were consciously cultivated in this circle. An untiring coworker of Philipp Manes was Dr. Merzbach, whom I often heard speak the part of Gretchen, and to whom I am grateful for much encouragement. The role of Faust was taken by the well-known actor and director Arnsfeld, whose lectures about his own travels by ship during the period when he had already been forbidden to perform in Germany were very well received.

Gradually, performances multiplied like mushrooms. They became more varied, more comfortable both for performers and for the audience. There were evenings when, if one came early—though breathing was difficult in the crowded room—one could, sitting on rough benches, listen and enjoy. One could choose concerts, theater (without scenery, of course), travelogues, scientific and literary lectures, evenings of ballads, and who knows what else. A large library was established, which, however, only those who were unable to work because of their age or sickness found time to visit. A concert hall was furnished; soon a second one was ready. Later, the SS supported these enterprises; in fact, they actually ordered these ventures, so they could brilliantly pass the inspections by the international commissions. The SS would be notified in advance of the programs, so that this freedom occurred within the limits of an outer restraint. Even a puppet theater was planned, to be under the direction of the talented young actor Raden. Dr. Merzbach had already suggested that I write a work for it. I started, but the puppet theater did not materialize, since a transport took away the men who were to build it. Raden, too, was one of them. Like all these transports, this one, too, led to death.

In the office of "free time activities" musical instruments were lent to musicians to make concerts possible. In an ante-room, a few young men sat day after day from morning till evening over the laborious task of copying out by hand the few pieces of sheet music that had been brought along so that an orchestra could use them. While standing in line in the barrack yard with our little soup pots—often for hours, while the hot sun beat down mercilessly or the cold froze feet into immovable lumps of ice—and waiting for the distribution of the eternally same midday meal, it could happen that above the starving crowd, above the pyre of mattresses which had to be burned so that the vermin would burn up with them, above the medieval-looking, tattered, limping shapes of hunger and groups of orderlies and pallbearers carrying stretchers, suddenly, out of an open window, like a lark, there would rise up the unrestrained, floating voice of a concert singer, who was not willing to bury her high aspirations under misery and constraint, and who practiced and sang and trilled in defiance of all violence and despair and the misery of her own soul.

Concerts brought me the greatest happiness. We lived in the land of the Czechs, to whom music is as natural an expression as language is to other people. One of the greatest—if not the greatest—was pianist Professor Bernhard Kaff. At his performances I felt as if stars showered down on us like tears shed by heaven over our misery. Kaff, this wonderful but modest artist, did not survive the war. Auschwitz devoured him. Next to him two other stars shone brightly: the women pianists Sommer-Herz and Edith Steiner-Krauss. Who could count them all! Magda Spiegel, the alto singer from Frankfurt, also perished in Auschwitz.

Where can I erect the memorial for the man whose lectures on music history, illustrated with musical performances, transported us so totally away from our time that we shook our heads afterward: Where are you really? Whose words provided us spiritual food for the following days and lived on in us, until his next lecture attracted hundreds of us again like a magnet? Where is your monument, Kurt Singer? Even today I still see you before me, your handsome masculine head with its thick silvery hair, your fiery eyes. What happened to you? Theresienstadt killed you; like so many thousands of other victims, it took you, too. It could not kill you entirely; in those few of us who saw freedom again, you live on.

Once when getting my meal, chance allotted me a place behind Kurt Singer. Ahead of us, two people were fighting— over a spoonful of soup or something like that, I can't remember anymore. "Yes, yes, people," he nodded in his cheerful, melancholy way, "something else has to be found."

There were times of horror and of darkness, when all these expressions were damned to silence, when all "free time activities" were forbidden. If large transports were leaving, if someone had—in the eyes of our tormentors—done something wrong or perhaps even had tried to escape at night, usually only to be found anyway and then to die even more gruesomely, then all programs were forbidden for some time, and a dead silence hung over the place.

The hours of spiritual freedom often cost very dearly. We hurried, dirty as we were, from work to the program, where we often arrived so late that getting in was out of the question. And if we were successful after all, it still was difficult enough. Our hungry stomachs did not want to quiet down, one's entire body trembled with weakness and nerves, and we were so indescribably tired, so worn down to the last particle of strength, that willpower and enthusiasm proved weak against the superior strength of sleep. One sat, therefore, one slept. One heard a fragment, fell asleep again, listened again, and so on. But when Kaff or Singer performed, I never slept. May angels sing to them as they sang to us.

But I wanted to speak about Philipp Manes. The room which he was allowed to use for his performances was more than wretched. At first it was a damp, dark, thick-walled, narrow partition in the barrack. Later, the tireless man went with his faithful group of artists to an attic in one of the old houses—the same attic in which those baptized Catholics and Protestants had celebrated their first Christmas in

Theresienstadt and which they had even decorated with a little tree with lights.

Philipp Manes was one of the best storytellers I have ever heard. He sat there, the old gentleman, shadowed by the darkness of his room, and spread the pictures of his extended travels out before us, the varied experiences—perhaps not more varied than the experiences of other people, but seen with such insightful eyes, kept alive in his mind, and brought to life again so vividly for us that it could only be *his* experiences—the hours then carried us away on broad wings. Later he put on splendid theater evenings; the actors, sitting around the table, only performed in front of the scenery of our imagination—but what matter! A performance of Rostand's *Cyrano de Bergerac* remains unforgettable for me; a good theater in a large city would not have been ashamed of it.

Toward the end of the time in Theresienstadt the old gentleman spent every free hour at his bare table up in the garret, which, with its modest triangular eyelike window, gave light to his ongoing work: He wrote a diary.

Everything that had happened during his long time there, his artistic work, the work of others, the people he met through his art: his pen captured everything in detailed reports. We always saw him writing, if we saw him at all. Often, in his absence, I left a little mug with wildflowers on his desk, which I had picked for him stealthily against regulations on the banks of the moat.

I do not think that anything survived of his reports and perhaps these lines are the only witness to his devoted activity. He surely took his writings with him, on the way from which nobody returned.

It may have been in the fall of 1943 that I took some of my poems to him, worried like a student. He put them into his writing case and nodded: "I will read them, as soon as I have time..."

I shared the room then with fifteen women and made friends with a Czech-Jewish woman of my age. Our opinions were often so opposed that we had arguments. But we always ended by embracing each other. Yet despite the difference of milieu in our upbringing and the resulting differences in our points of view, there glowed in us the same fervor for everything beautiful and great in people, and for the unknown from where it streams down to us. It is almost impossible to imagine that someone could bear as much suffering as this woman did. But she had not even now reached the end of the path of her fate. In the same house, in a room for men, on the other side of the balustrade, lived her paralyzed husband. He trembled for her, she had a heart ailment; she trembled for him, he was paralyzed. Often, she took my hand and led me to him: "Here, sit down, read your poems to my husband." And I sat down on the edge of the rough bunk bed and started.

When the face of poor Mr. Mahler, distorted by illness and deprivation, suddenly took on a little color, and when with stiff lips he ponderously tried to form words: "Please, one more time—please, read it again," then for half a day my

View of the train station in Theresienstadt-Bauschowitz taken during the arrival of a transport of Dutch Jews in February 1944. (Ivan Vojtech Fric, courtesy of the United States Holocaust Memorial Museum [USHMM] Photo Archives)

Arrival of Jews into the Theresienstadt ghetto. After a grueling transport, prisoners had to walk the last several miles from the train station to the camp. (Courtesy of USHMM Photo Archives)

At the entrance to Theresienstadt, the sign read, "Work sets you free." This slogan was part of the Nazi systematic deceit, used to hide their true intentions from the Jews. (Ghetto Fighters' House—Beit Lohamei Haghetaot)

A transport of Dutch Jews arrives in Theresienstadt in February 1944. Carrying all of their belongings, they make their way through an archway into the ghetto. (Ivan Vojtech Fric, courtesy of USHMM Photo Archives)

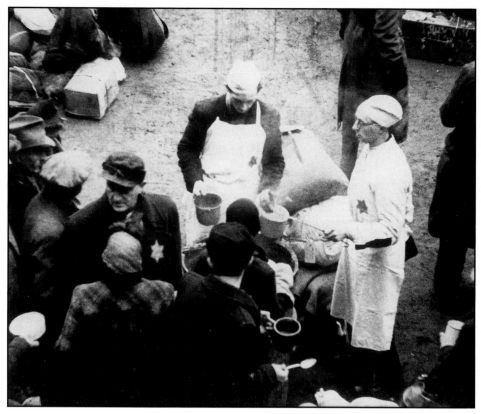

A prisoner wearing a cook's uniform dishes out food to the newly arrived prisoners in a transport of Dutch Jews, February 1944. (Ivan Vojtech Fric, courtesy of USHMM Photo Archives)

Money used in the ghetto. Worthless paper bills were issued by the Nazis for the imprisoned Jews. These bills replaced genuine money that the Jews were forbidden to use in the ghetto. (Ghetto Fighters' House—Beit Lohamei Haghetaot)

A staged street view with people in the ghetto. Gerty Spies tells of a beautification project to impress visiting commissions to Theresienstadt. Buildings along a selected route were painted and refurbished and other improvements made to show "normal" life in the ghetto. (YIVO Institute for Jewish Research, courtesy of USHMM Photo Archives)

The reality of life in Theresienstadt. Men, women, and children prisoners in a muddy courtyard near a barrack. At its peak, 53,004 people were living in an area of only 125,770 square yards. (YIVO Institute for Jewish Research, courtesy of USHMM Photo Archives)

Prisoners collecting food rations. Rations were strictly regulated and the quality of the food poor. Starvation, exhaustion, and disease caused the death of nearly 33,000 prisoners in Theresienstadt. (YIVO Institute for Jewish Research, courtesy of USHMM Photo Archives)

Women prepare food under trees in a muddy area near the remains of furniture. Gerty Spies described her quarters as having "no furniture, no oven, no stove." (YIVO Institute for Jewish Research, courtesy of USHMM Photo Archives)

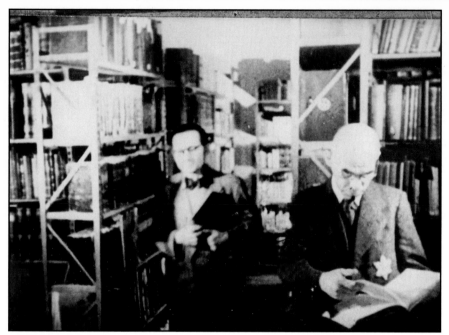

The Theresienstadt ghetto library, whose books had been confiscated from arriving prisoners. The library was heavily used, although the prisoners' state of exhaustion often interfered with their reading. Facilities such as this library helped create the "positive" image of the ghetto. (Ghetto Fighters' House—Beit Lohamei Haghetaot)

A laborer lowers the corpse of an inmate into a common grave. Prayers for the dead were said at graveside by surviving family members. According to one survivor, all able-bodied men had to serve as grave diggers until they were given other work in the ghetto. (Yad Vashem Photo Archives, courtesy of USHMM Photo Archives)

Corpses being carted to the crematorium at the Theresienstadt-Bohusov Hollow. Built in 1942, the crematorium was used to save the expense of coffins. According to one survivor, the ashes of the deceased were kept in cardboard boxes. Before the end of the war, the SS had the ashes dumped in a nearby river. (Terezin Memorial Museum, courtesy of USHMM Photo Archives)

Deportation from Theresienstadt to Auschwitz. Two faces look out; one hand is waving from the opening of a freight car. About 88,000 were transported to the death camps in the East, usually to Auschwitz. (Yad Vashem Photo Archives, courtesy of USHMM Photo Archives)

First photos taken in the ghetto after being liberated by the Soviet army, which took place on May 8, 1945. Prisoners line the street to greet their liberators. (Yad Vashem Photo Archives, courtesy of USHMM Photo Archives)

A few elderly survivors are seen enjoying a sunny day after liberation. Trees and the long barracks of Theresienstadt can be seen in the background. (Ghetto Fighters' House—Beit Lohamei Haghetaot)

doubts disappeared: Is it not self-deception with which you seek to imagine yourself past this time of horror? And I was as grateful to him as he was to me.

Picking Up Food

I go and pick up my noonday meal,
In my hand I hold two empty bowls,
A piece of paper with name and numbers,
The name blue, the numbers red.

Small are the bowls, yet too large.
On the way, gray shadows beg:
"Say, will you keep the soup yourself?"
I pass them, only nodding.

I take it—why not!—
It is so water-thin and scanty.
So measured and paltry
Is the spare main meal, too.

I retreat to somewhere
Hidden from the animals of hunger,
Who stare at my every bite
With helpless gaping.

My Years in Theresienstadt

The spoon scrapes up the last bit.
The hunger was not to be conquered dead,
No!—Laughing, it clambers back
And triumphs and sits tight!

The imagination is terrified awake
Hands start to search;
Is there not a small dried-up piece of cake,
Has not a small piece of bread hidden itself somewhere?

And finally, nature helps me:
I sleep.—And my eyes see
A paradise created by desire—
Only for ten short minutes.

The autumn of 1943 threw hundreds of women together in the west barracks. I found myself in a new world, among strange faces, and must admit that I was afraid at the realization: Here on the whole, you will come into contact with beings more coarse than ever before. We were twenty-five in one room, lying on top of and next to one another, and in this confinement, we all suffered from the presence of our roommates. In the evening friends and relatives visited; the shack echoed and reverberated with the babble, from chopping wood and other activities. My eyes clouded over, my ears were ringing. And once all visitors had left, at 9:00 P.M., the women lay on their narrow plank beds and the conversation started up again, back and forth, until finally tiredness conquered even these tongues.

Luckily, I did not know that I would have to spend one-and-a-half years here. The stay in this room was one of the most merciless trials of nerves in my life. I went to work early and came back at night dead tired, and my nerves were so jumpy that I could not sleep. My fists on my ears, or holding my head so it would not burst, I sat on the edge of my sleeping cot, saw the hours of the night disappear like ghosts, and—created poetry. My good angel did not forsake me even here.

Not that all the other women in this room were insufferable gossips. The deprivation, tortures, and psychological torments to which we were helplessly subjected had different effects on its victims. Many lost their nerve, and there were hours when they did not know themselves. There were many gradations, from calm, heroic dignity to total breakdown in despair, and only a few were so disciplined that they did not have their weak hour from time to time.

There were two women among us whom I would like to recall. They were friends, and slept next to each other on the second level of the so-called three-story bunk bed, which consisted of a wooden frame to hold six people. Many an evening, after all the others were finally quiet, these two were still whispering, telling each other what had happened that day. The older one, Dr. Martin, though a German, had come from Holland. She was an anthropologist, a serious, many-faceted, well-educated person. She had white hair and a thin, fine face; she was always friendly, well-balanced, and interested in everything concerning people. Her neighbor, Flora Heidingsfelder, was from Frankfurt. She seemed to me an almost supernatural being. The dignity with which these two women endured hunger and all other injustices, even their fears, became a great example for the rest of us. They never complained, they accepted quietly and calmly all changes and knowingly shared the smallest possessions even with people whom they knew to be, by some stroke of luck, better provided for than they were.

Flora Heidingsfelder—called Heidi for short—a delicate woman who was always cold, and because of malnutrition often had heart problems, never received a package, except once. If one had relatives in a foreign country, and if they knew of the arrangement, they could transmit money to a firm in Portugal, so that it could send a small package with groceries to Theresienstadt. And if this package was not stolen on the way, or stolen or plundered in Theresienstadt, then, one day we would be told we could pick it up.

It was a great day for Heidi. She asked me to accompany her to the post office. She was so happy, and could hardly believe that now even she would be one of the lucky ones. Sardines, dates, figs from Portugal! Her face beamed: we hurried back to the barrack. I turned away at once, so that she could enjoy her bounty undisturbed. But what happened? Heidi opened it, unpacked it, and beaming with joy, without a moment of hesitation, she shared the contents of her only package with the twenty-five women in the room.

During the winter I spent in these barracks, I had my first encounter with one of the most important men that life led into my circle. Hans Friedländer, from Vienna, a child of that city in the best sense, had been lieutenant field marshal and advisor to the emperor, had fought—like so many comrades of his fate—in World War I, and now he, too, was in Theresienstadt. For his outstanding merits as a leader of the heroic defense of Karst he had been given the rank of lieutenant field marshal and had been titled—but he did not permit this form of address, and was known popularly and simply as "the general." As a so-called half-Jew he would not have been deported. Since his Jewish wife, however, received her orders one day, he volunteered to accompany her. It was to be his death.

Never have I met a person who embodied the expression "luminous personality" better than this man with his natural amiability, the pairing of manliness with a most engaging Viennese charm. United in him were both a sparkling mind with a deeply religious joy for life, and masculinity in this word's best and most noble meaning. Always and everywhere he found the right word, the right tone. There was no situation in which he lost his humor. The basis for the rare balance may have been his deep religious tranquility, which in firmness and humility combined the dignity of an educated mind with the warm heart of a good comrade. All this made him one of the most popular personalities in camp. He was blessed with good looks; a full head of hair framed his clear features, his shining, sunlike eyes; his tall figure never showed any weariness; his nature expressed once again a world of chivalric charm which has been pushed into the shadows in our brutal times. Peace-loving down to the most insignificant disagreements within our exhausting day-to-day life in Theresienstadt, he actually relished facing danger openly and simply. With all his vivacity, he leaned toward the spiritual. His lectures on history drew hundreds of people of all classes and kept their attention. One of these lecture evenings, which took as its theme "The last century of the papacy," signified one of the high points to this demanding audience of Theresienstadt.

He made the mistake of keeping a diary, and—since his notes were of a nonpolitical nature—of not making a secret of it to the Gestapo, which liked to take the Commission* to the "House for Prominent People." As a consequence, in the fall of 1944, he had to leave the camp with one of the large transports on "special orders." A few hours before his removal, within the circle of close friends, he gave another moving lecture.

When, against the rules, I went to see him in the so-called sluice, he looked at me calmly: "How often have I faced death! In speech and in writing I have defended my belief. I would despise myself if now I started shaking. Work. Give to humanity what is your gift to give." He embraced me, and breathed a kiss on my forehead.

His departing words to Mrs. Elsa: "I cannot pretend to be a figure of courage all year round and then, when it matters, fall apart."

What this man gave to me—the stimulation, suggestions, and self-confidence—cannot be acknowledged adequately. This is my way of expressing my gratitude to him. He used to say, "Child, the best thing about your poetry is that you have read very little. This gives you your natural naïveté."

It was he who held the first small gathering to give me the

---

*The International Red Cross Commission visited the camp in 1944 (see Introduction, p. 14).

opportunity to recite my poems. It started with very few people in the so-called Kumbal. This was a very small room, over-crowded with his two roommates. Their bunk beds climbed up one wall and almost reached the one opposite. Despite that, six of us found room. And I read. Not without reward. The "host," Dr. Helfreich (he deserved his name),* worked in the food supply department, and I returned to my world of the barracks—difficult to believe—with a roll and a slice of sausage.

This first reading attracted attention. I was still working as a stoker in the mica workshop, but after the next transport left a gaping hole in this operation, it was unexpectedly halted on "higher orders." They had run out of material and apparently there was not enough interest to provide more. A sigh of relief went through our ranks. For a few days, we were allowed a rest, until the work was reorganized. We were assigned to do different jobs in the camp operation. I became a so-called orderly in the Children's Welfare Office. They had chosen me because I knew how to take care of stoves. Heating, cleaning, carrying coal and water, as well as doing messenger service—that was my job now.

The second winter tried our patience with the torture of homesickness, fear, and deprivations. Even the horrors had a rhythm of their own: transports that came—transports that left—into the impenetrable darkness, in whose abyss the eternal question lurked: What next? January 1944 brought my uncle, my mother's brother, to Theresienstadt with a transport from Frankfurt.

---

*The name Helfreich translates into "rich-of-help" or "always-ready-to-help."

My Years in Theresienstadt

This beloved uncle, Dr. Robert Kahn, who had worked for many years as assistant and then as head of the Ehrlich Biological Institute in Frankfurt, could have boasted that he was the codeveloper of Salvarsan. But he did not boast. In his modesty, he did not find time to think about himself. One could characterize him as follows: "Love is to help in spite of everything." He had learned from life to reduce his expectations to a minimum, and he was proof that people can, nevertheless—or perhaps because of this insight—do good out of conviction without asking questions, sometimes with just a shrug of the shoulders.

His inexhaustible knowledge—jokingly I used to call him "my encyclopedia"—complemented his character and actions. His character was as simple and plain as his knowledge was profound. How calmly he integrated himself from the first day into life in camp must have been obvious to anyone looking for examples of quiet heroism. He was here, it was to be so; he accepted it and tried to help.

Immediately after his arrival, I tried to arrange a room for him in the "House for Prominent People." Perhaps things would have turned out differently—but what an effort to convince this modest person that it was his right! Finally, months later, I succeeded in getting him to submit a petition and to write his biography, as required by the authorities. In the meantime, he lived in the attic of an old house, with untold other unlucky victims, where his care for others hastened his end.

When he, who aside from being a prominent scientist also was a productive poet, for the first time looked at one of my short works—it was a description born of homesickness for his hometown Edenkoben—a devout suspense took hold of me as he pushed his glasses to his forehead and started reading, and I followed the melancholy smile with which he returned in his mind to his home and thought to himself with quiet joy, "Our family heritage has not yet died out." He seemed fairly happy with me. When I had done my best under the circumstances to assure his physical well-being with whatever primitive comfort there was, then, first thing, I introduced him to Mrs. Elsa.

We entered the room, and I was touched to see that the blind woman had picked from the few belongings which camp life had left her a somewhat better dress than she usually wore. Though she herself could not see, she wanted to give pleasure to the eye of her visitor.

It happened as I expected: after a few minutes I was superfluous. But now I had spiritual parents who watched over my creations.

I learned much from my uncle; from our many exchanges I received intellectual stimulation, to which I attribute the creation of several humorous poems. Unfortunately, his own poetic writings had become victim of a bombing attack in Frankfurt, and whatever he wrote in camp is illegible because of a tremor of his right hand. (I rescued these pages, but they are simply undecipherable documents.)

If I wanted to make sure not to miss my uncle, I looked for him at Mrs. Elsa's. One short evening hour remains unforgettable. After work I stormed somewhat brusquely into the seclusion of their reading hour, which they had made a regular event, wresting it away in defiance of all powers of despair inherent in our condition. They did not like to be disturbed. Once they realized, however, that I simply could not keep my rhymes composed during the last two nights to myself any longer, they smilingly put their hands into their laps and listened to me.

I cannot remember what I read first; it was either "The Dwarfs' Sunday," a fairy tale of the forest which describes the high-spirited joys of a community of dwarfs on a summer Sunday; or perhaps it was "The Miller's Way Home," which was as eerily serious as the other one was exuberantly joyful. In any case, I think the two did not regret sacrificing their happy island of solitude, and our conversation afterward was stimulating and extensive, so that we had to hurry to get "home" before curfew time in Theresienstadt.

"Is this the first ballad you have written?" my uncle asked, referring to "The Miller's Way Home."

"What is a ballad?" I could only ask in response.

"You do not know that? Oh, so much the better," he said with his melancholy smile.

From "The Dwarfs' Sunday":

> *To keep Sunday special, to honor guests,*
> *We made roast of ant in its own juice,*
> *After that, aphid milk puree over elderbush berries*
> *And pollen wine of untold force.*
> *To finish off, a cigar from whortleberry leaves*
> *And then the climbing of the castle tower.*

How I Survived It

This castle had been, many years ago,
An oak tree, powerful and large.
Then lightning had hit its crown.
Now it stood broken and black through and through,
The stump surrounded with humming of bumblebees.
The night ghost of the count of dwarfs inhabited it....

From "The Miller's Way Home":

> *He walked, counting to himself*
> *Along old, well-known paths.*
> *The richness strained his mind—*
> *Then it slid toward him.*
>
> *It crawled out of a hollow tree;*
> *It wriggled nimbly,*
> *Flowing through the moon's pale space*
> *To where the forest stopped.*
>
> *The miller was a real man,*
> *He did not know fear.*
> *But here, horror took hold of him,*
> *He looked for his stick.*
>
> *He swung wide—and hit the mark.*
> *Ha! how the pieces flew.*
> *But in the air—the spook was powerful*
> *They melted together....*

My Years in Theresienstadt

In those days it began to be dangerous to write. The inspections, the searching of our houses increased. Several painters whose pictures of Theresienstadt were found during a search by the SS—due to the carelessness of a prisoner—had to pay for their courage either with the transport or with their lives. What to do? My roommates advised me, my friend Herta implored me, to bury or even to burn the written evidence of my camp experience. I could not bring myself to do it. To bury—that would mean to let it decay, and to burn it—that I really could not do. To leave the pages unwatched in the room during the hours of work meant to put the others in danger. No hiding place was safe. And so it happened that I went to work every day with a heavy travel bag over my shoulders, and at night I switched between different hiding places—between wall and plank, at the bottom of a knapsack, in a sack of straw—and in the morning I recovered them and took them with me. This I did every day, until the day of liberation. And luck was with me.

My supervisor looked at my habit with unspoken suspicion. Why did I always have this bag? One day before I left work she ordered me to open it to let her see whether I had stolen buttons and hooks or such things. I obeyed at once, with mocking satisfaction. "Why do you carry this rubbish back and forth!" she yelled flabbergasted and looked at me as if I had fallen from the moon.

Because of carrying packages, water, and coal, I got an inflammation of my knee. I had to stay in bed. That was the end of my career at the Welfare Office for Children. While I was slowly recovering, I saw my uncle's face turn paler and paler. His seventy-five years could not tolerate this hunger, these deprivations. On April 10, 1944, after three months of imprisonment, a merciful heart attack released him from the terror of Theresienstadt (and from the torture of his house elder, who ordered him to do heavy physical work despite his ruptured hernia. This, too, sadly, must be said).

The day after his death I met the man who worked on processing petitions for admission to the "House for Prominent People."

"I forwarded the petition. It should not be too much longer."

"It is too late."

Thank God, spring came. I did not have to look desperately—with nerves ready to tear—for an empty corner to be alone. Now I could lie down on the sparse meadow by the rampart and let my gaze roam across the small trickle which crept muddily in the moat. Many came here, and yet one could be alone, even if it was only for a quarter of an hour.

Spring brought with it two changes. My companions elected me to the post of room elder, despite my resistance. And uncannily, Theresienstadt was being subjected to a beautification project. What did that mean? To be sure, they had previously put in a sewer system, had torn down walls, and had built barracks. But now they started to paint houses, to build pavilions, and to decorate the whole place with magnificent flower-beds. Anxious, busy activity filled the small alleys as if it all had to be finished by tomorrow. Once again, wild, hopeful rumors buzzed from mouth to mouth. Would Theresienstadt come under the supervision of the Red

Cross? Would the SS leave? Had the time arrived? No, but no! Soon we realized: it was for the Commission, all for the Commission. Theresienstadt became an exhibit, and we ourselves were to be the objects exhibited. This was not something new, only this time it was done more extravagantly than before. Heaven knew why, but much seemed to depend on it. Now we could walk through the streets with hungry stomachs and stop at "butcher shops" with display windows crammed full with meat and sausage, or we could be enchanted looking at flaming rose-beds, without being allowed to touch them or even bend over them to drink in their scent. New longings were awakened, new Tantalus-like torments conjured up. And these, too, could be transformed within and given shape. They merged with the burning evening sky and with the view onto the improbability of the world outside. Over there, on the faraway country highway that divided the fields like a parting, we saw strangers we had never met, would never meet, saw them on their bicycles, saw the farmers troop to the little town in small caravans, saw women push perambulators, and saw cars stir up dust in the streets. We could not hear any of this—it was too far away to reach our ears. All the more improbable, all the more like a dream. It was mixed in with the sweet torments of homesickness, which, like an insidious illness, had settled at the base of our soul. All this together stirred and took shape in me and urgently sought outward form.

Together with the beautification project, our cultural presentations were again promoted—and required. Watercolors of Theresienstadt graced the freshly painted, dank walls of the Magdeburg barracks. At the entrance gate, where every stone, if it had a voice, would have had to scream out loud about all the misery it had seen, hung lovely hand-painted flower idylls, and they were also boastingly displayed behind the panes of the deceitful display windows.

The same children who, under threats on the lives of their fathers or mothers, had been prohibited from picking up even one chestnut in the park, on whose young faces and in whose sad eyes the habit of denial was already painted, to whom all schooling had been denied, these children, under the supervision of their educators, put on an exhibition of their own drawings, handiworks, woodcarvings, sculptures, and first literary attempts, which astonished visitors admired.

The room elder has to be always ready—my thoughts always wanted to be alone. This opposition gave my existence a certain tension, a peculiar fascination. To carry bread, pull carts through the mud, scrub floors—and to lie by the moat, to dream after the swallows above the roofs, and to write.

It was only for a short while. On orders of the commandant's office, many of the room elders had to be dismissed, and I was one of them. Good. Now came other work.

One of the seven relatives I buried in Theresienstadt, my uncle Richard Hirsch from Berlin, had left me as his legacy an acquaintance with Martha Geissmar, a violin player about forty years old, whose name I cannot write down without being moved by feelings of tender friendship. Martha found a new job for me: I became an orderly for her boss, Dr. Jacob Jacobson.

Jacobson had to fulfill one of the strangest duties a Jew was ever ordered to do by the SS: he did Jewish genealogical research. German thoroughness: there was an office of Aryan genealogical research—so there had to be one for Jewish genealogical research, too. That incidentally those giving the orders were also "entrusted with" the destruction of the last representatives of this ethnic group whose names, written in decorative letters, were to fill the folios made of pig leather—well, that had nothing to do with the research.

Jacobson had worked on this in Berlin, and had been sent into exile with his books to continue working on it. He sat in a tiny room into which daylight found entrance only indirectly and with difficulty; he turned the pages, he read, with his myopic eyes he bent closely, very closely over the pages; he wrote and dictated and—he did good.

He was a little afraid of the new orderly. A "bluestocking" who was to clean his room, scrub his floor, do errands, scare away bugs—how would that work out? But we buried our fears quickly on the first morning under mutual laughter, and soon we were good friends. On my second day he happened to ask me, "Can you dash off an occasional poem for me?" I sat down—and it worked, and it was Martha who was most pleased. Despite our misery the three of us spent some happy hours together. If the doctor went out—in order to fulfill his duties, he was allowed to live alone in this dark room made for dwarfs—he gave the key to the orderly; then she sat at his desk—at last a quiet spot in the midst of the dance of death in Theresienstadt. What—aside from his goodness—made Jacobson so blessed was his capacity for joy, his humor. When he told how he had traveled all through Germany in his youth, we forgot where we were.

During the early summer months of 1944, my position enabled me to start work on the puppet play that Mrs. Merzbach had suggested to me.

While I carried the small notes from my boss through dark courtyards and up the stairs of barracks, while I dragged cleaning buckets and mattresses upstairs and downstairs, bright pictures of fairy tales were formed in my head for this, my first attempt, "The Lantern"—the completion and performance of which we celebrated with the consumption of a package Martha had received from home. Luckily, the contents had not been stolen.

Thus throughout this summer I starved and wrote. The bugs bred so rapidly in our barracks that we had to spend our nights outside. Every night we carried our bedding outside, and put it on the gravel paths between the lawn and flowerbeds on which we were not allowed to step because of the beautification project. A fantastic gypsy world opened up. I lay there, night after night, the full gaze of the stars above me; slept very little; saw the face of the moon change, waning and waxing; heard and saw the night wind roar, shaking and bending the trees; and felt closer to nature and its forces than ever despite all constraints. Let hunger gnaw, if it wanted—I dismissed all that was oppressive and surrendered myself to the consolation in nature. These nights were a remedy, and it could not have been planned more beneficially. Here poems originated which I kept in my head despite my tiredness until I had time to write them down.

I was not easy to get along with during that time; I had retreated into my own world, and this made me obstinate and unapproachable. Conversations with others became a torture to me, and I often admired my friends Herta Levi and Martha Geissmar, who patiently endured my changes of temper and tried as much as they could to make my life easier.

Both are not alive any longer.

Herta Levi was from Munich. Her husband, Hans, had worked for the Munich Jewish Community Service until it was disbanded during the summer of 1943. They had come to Theresienstadt with the last transport from there. This transport had not been assembled in Camp Milbertshofen like the other transports from Munich and then continued on. Rather, the few people left had been thrown into the prison at the police headquarters until departure, men separated from women.

Herta had not wanted to go. She had wanted to end her life, as many others had done before her. But Hans was a life-affirming optimist—nonsense, they would both survive and return. At last they came to an agreement: they would pulverize the pills which Herta knew how to obtain and smuggle them in her purse, declaring them as saccharine, if necessary.

The smuggling succeeded. But when they were pulverizing them, the small glass tube broke; Hans hurt himself. It was an insignificant cut to his little finger, and he did not pay attention to it. During the days and nights of their imprisonment in the police station, neither sheets nor medicine were permitted, and the little wound became inflamed. His companions demanded a doctor, the supervisor tried, but to no avail—no medical help was allowed.

When Herta—on the way to Theresienstadt—saw her

husband, she did not recognize him. And the same happened to me. In the courtyard of the Hohenelber barracks—we called them "Hohenelbe" for short—under beautiful, old chestnut trees, there was a military hospital barrack. When I entered the room in which Hans was supposed to be, I looked from one bed to the other, but I did not see him until an ancient man—Hans was not forty-four yet—waved at me from one of the corners. It was Hans.

He fought death for three weeks. Blood transfusions—the fever went down. The next day it was up again. The infection went on, kept spreading—it was too late. In his delirium he saw an airplane on his last day, which was to take him to freedom. "Hurry, Hurry," he called to Herta. "They are leaving any minute! Oh my God, we can't get on," he lamented.

We were allowed to accompany the funeral procession only to the barricade. From there the vehicle, loaded down with coffins, swayed unescorted toward Bauschowitz—to the crematorium. Herta collapsed onto one of the cut-down trees lying on the road: "My husband, who wanted to fetch the stars from the sky for me—how can he leave me—so alone!"

We had been good acquaintances until then; now the experience of Hans's death brought us together as good friends.

Later on, Herta worked as a secretary in the Magdeburger barracks. There she sometimes had the opportunity to type one or more of my poems on a clean sheet of paper. Printed characters on a white rectangle—they seemed much more credible than when written by hand on a piece of packing paper.

My Years in Theresienstadt

Martha Geissmar was the daughter of Jacob Geissmar, a councillor of the Higher Regional Court who had lived most recently (together with his wife) in Munich. When I met Martha, he had already died from the deprivations in Theresienstadt. Martha had spent her childhood in Heidelberg; her parents had raised her in the Protestant faith. Later her music studies brought her to Berlin, where she often socialized in Jewish homes; she developed a lively interest in the belief of her ancestors and returned to the Jewish faith.

Martha was tall, slender, good-looking, with soft clear features. Her cheerfulness made being together with her a source of peace. Shortly before our first meeting she had just gotten over a head cold that was going around in camp at that time, and she was still very weak. She was released from work for a while, and she suggested that we should meet at the bank of the moat whenever I had even one free hour and tell each other about our past lives. She had experienced so little happiness, and I wished so very much that at least some of her wishes would be fulfilled. We became friends quickly, but our friendship did not last even half a year.

During the summer of 1944, Manes organized a contest for poets, and without my knowing it, he entered the poems I had left with him. I found out that I was one of the winners. An evening was chosen when all the winners would read their own poems. Long before the set time the attic was filled with listeners. The podium had been decorated with the modest resources of the camp. The audience sat on rough benches way back to the attic stairs; all the way back in the slanting corners, between openings and beams, stood those who could not find a seat. Behind the podium there were benches for the speakers, who initially stayed in the background. We could observe a tension in our audience, just as before a major event; the searing heat of the day, which still filled the room in these evening hours and made breathing difficult, could not chase away our guests.

At last our friend Manes climbed onto the wooden throne. He welcomed with a few words those who had come to give and those who had come to take. He went on briefly about his plan to let "my poets," as he so kindly and sincerely called us, recite one after the other, and then finally he distributed slips of paper to the audience on which they were to note what and whom they had liked best. It was to be a referendum as to whose voice could warm the listeners' hearts best.

The prizes were distributed. There were ten of us. Each of us received a book with a dedication and a diploma signed personally by the highest judge, Professor Utitz, and by our patron and friend, Manes. Even today I can still feel the solemn excitement with which I climbed the few steps when it was my turn, and the emotion with which I accepted the book. Manes's handshake accompanying it was an expression of his friendship, across all the horrors of the times, a spiritual bond over which death has no power.

Now the main event was to follow—but there was an unpleasant surprise. Probably on orders from our tormentors, the administration for "free time activity" had mandated at the last minute that only poems which had been awarded a prize could be heard by our listeners. These poems had already passed the sieve of censorship and their political content had been examined and found unobjectionable. For me and some others that turned out to be disadvantageous. Our poems that Manes had entered were older and we had meanwhile written more powerful ones. Also, some of the prize poems were not as well suited for recitation—they were meant to be read. Therefore we declined to come forward, and were satisfied with listening.

The performances varied. Many did not go beyond description of our everyday life in prison, yet were in part so powerful and moving in their simplicity that they achieved a sense of freedom after all. There were poetic nature descriptions—sometimes too detailed, torturing our nerves—and general lyrical themes. Two of the prizewinners were women, myself and Mrs. Ilse Weber, from Prague, who unfortunately recited her good poem too shyly. One of the best we heard came from the Viennese cabaretist Leo Strauss (son of Oskar Strauss), who—also like Ilse Weber—together with thousands who shared her fate, suffered death by gassing only a few months later.

In the meantime, our barrack elder had noticed me. Perner was an enthusiastic supporter and patron of the arts as far as the circumstances in Theresienstadt allowed. Several times he let me use his workroom to hold recital evenings. The first one was a triple festivity for me. It happened on June 6, the birthday of my daughter. Moreover, after waiting for months and listening to bad news about extended bombing attacks in Munich, this day finally brought mail from home again. Lastly, at the same time, the for us almost inconceivable news of the landing of the Allied forces in France had filtered through the tight net of our isolation. A hopeful mood took hold of us and gave me the right stimulus for my recital.

This successful performance increased my delight in creativity. Without express approval only gatherings of up to thirty people were allowed. Anything larger had to be reported. But I really had no ambition to go outside the circle of my acquaintances. The more inconspicuous, the better. But nobody noticed that my audience unexpectedly surpassed this number. During the course of the summer, this program was repeated twice.

The hope-inspiring rumors increased: an attempt on Hitler's life! He received a small burn, to be sure, but he got away with his life. The Allied troops marched ever deeper into the country. They begrudged us this news, for us so heartening, but the secret friendship between some of the Czech gendarmes on guard duty and the Czech-Jewish camp inmates was as reliable as newspapers (or even more reliable). Even hidden in the small packages from home, on the bottom of a bag of flour or baked within a cake, we found delirium-inducing announcements of the progress toward our liberation. If only we might live to see it.

Like lightning out of the clear blue sky, the unforeseen order surprised us: "Start up the mica workshops. Beginning September 1—mica work again." And this time production was started on a grand scale. These last nine months were to exhaust all the bodily and spiritual strength that these bitter years had left still within us. Daily we died many a death from the torments of our souls, from fear, from bodily over-exertion and spiritual oppression. And yet each woman and girl who was part of the mica work process was in fact very lucky. For soon thereafter a number of mass transports to Auschwitz started such as Theresienstadt had never experienced before. Thousands and thousands more got their orders for departure—we did not know to where—and under a firm, brilliant blue fall sky the preparations for these horrible mass murders were played out. Workers in the mica workshop were exempted from the transports, of course, only if the desired output was realized.

When fear of death, when threat of transport hangs over you, you learn to work. To be punctual to the second, no, to be early, not to lift your head, not to look away from your work, to concentrate your thoughts on this most dull, monotonous business which required absolutely no thought, just in order not to waste motion, just to split one more mica-slate, to be able to point to the required number of grams at weighing— all that so as not to be part of the next transport like thousands of our companions in misfortune. Sweat poured, the heart beat hammerlike, hunger was gnawing—and our hands flew.

There were no free days, only changing shifts. Only a few hours were our own between sleep and work, between work and sleep, to lie by the water at the moat and to rest, unless we helped some other dear person pack, who was on her way to destruction. And this time the transports cleared out the city—Theresienstadt was empty. The streets so quiet, the houses so quiet. Our steps echoed. Our room also grew emptier. But who could be happy about space, considering how it was achieved? We all knew who paid for it.

Herta Levi was deported on one of these first transports. Shortly thereafter, it was Martha Geissmar's mother, and then Martha herself. Her precious violin, which she had smuggled miraculously into camp, and about whose survival she was almost more concerned than about her life, was left behind in camp; it fell into the wrong hands and was lost.

Seldom did I see a more sorrowful parting than Martha's. It was with a gentle, knowing melancholy that she distanced herself from life and people, disappointed by both.

"You are the only person I am grieving for," she repeatedly said. We parted in the evening in the pitch-black street. "So—farewell," she said softly and kissed me.

Heidi also went to her death with one of these fall transports.

This is how I lost my friends.

There is no need to tell how impossible it was to meditate in those times. If the mind was engaged, out of necessity the mechanism of moving the hands was slowed down. There-fore, writing became superfluous. Only during the rare free hours were some poor thoughts compressed into bitter-humorous comments about our existence as mica-workers, insignificant little things which sometimes helped my com-panions to pass the difficult hours of forced work. This is how the third winter of imprisonment passed.

Even our last few hours of free time were taken away from us. Most of the male workers had been deported to Auschwitz. Spring arrived. From other camps starved human skeletons who were even worse off than we were chased into our camp. They could not produce at all. We had to work for them. It meant we women had to do men's work. Our free time was taken up with it. Friends helped me so I could spend my free time in a suffocating potato cellar, from which I was allowed to take home a few potatoes each day. The basement was beneath a barrack. One stumbled from the courtyard down into it. The basement supervisor installed me as a guard at the door.

Only God knows how I survived this time. The war was near its end. The innumerable concentration camps situated in Germany—we had no conception of their total num-bers—were captured by the advancing Allied troops coming from the east and the west, but were emptied beforehand by the SS. The inmates, who had been tortured and starved for years, were chased further by the thousands on the insecure highways which were constantly bombarded and fired upon, to be gathered up in the last corner not yet occupied. This corner was Theresienstadt. The crowds of devastated shadowy apparitions which were driven together here carried with them epidemics; they were crammed into the barracks and turrets. Among them were beings who had long ago lost all their bearings and could not be distinguished from those innocently damned; all of them together were one gray heap of misery. They killed each other for a piece of bread.

A great many of these people lived in the Hannover barracks, where I did my potato duty. They prowled around the courtyard hungrily and noisily, lying in wait for a chance to get at something edible. When after culling, the buds, peelings, and decaying potatoes were carried upstairs from the basement in baskets or barrels to be emptied into pits, then these human animals crawled into the pits on all fours, let the garbage rain on top of them, and ate, insensibly, whatever they could get their hands on, unaware of their surroundings. The supervisors had a hopeless task to make them give this up. Only when their hunger abated did it stop.

Well, these shadow human beings realized very soon why I stood there. They tried to sneak around me, push me aside, strike me, to get into the basement. I stood like an archangel, motionless, armed with an iron pole, and saw myself confronted with the relentless question: How will you—a woman—cope with these lurking figures of horror?

When I could not think of another remedy, I hit upon the idea of using the power of my gaze as a weapon. I made it a habit to look into these lurking eyes, actually, to look through them, without the person quite realizing it. They may have thought I was staring ahead of me, absentminded, and only by chance into their unsteady, greedy, predatorlike eyes as well. And the miracle happened—I could stop them with this glance. A circle of constraint formed around me, they retreated. Late at night, I fell on my cot dead tired and robbed of my last strength.

But in the evening hours, after this dance of ghosts had retreated to the rooms in the barracks, and when the courtyard was quiet and empty before me, I found time to capture my impressions and to write them down hastily before I fell asleep. When later—I had long since left there—with the arrival of the liberating troops, the potato basement suddenly was opened up, the whole gang—I cannot remember how many there were—plunged down the stairs, broke into the basement, simply trampled down the woman who administered it, and cleaned it out. A quarter of an hour later, not a single small potato could be found.

On the whole—how could it have been otherwise—these days by their nature did not allow for writing. Horror overcame us, shook us, and ate into our very soul. It was a nice little stimulus to see one of my humorous mica-poems—the so-called mica-legend—illustrated by a friend, Alexander Gutfeld. This many talented person, who had lost his left leg and his right arm during the First World War, painted with so much charm and sympathy—one could not ask for more.

During this, the most agitating time of my imprisonment, I still had one quiet source of joy: it was the sight of the old, humpbacked, but picturesque houses and backyards of this little town, which I had not been allowed to leave in three years even for one day, and with which my senses and habits were closely entwined. I was so familiar with the area that I could have walked almost any path with my eyes closed. But I kept them open, and enjoyed consciously all the hidden beauty of the magically decaying scenery, which shaped the background of a world of tears and desperation.

It is not my task to recount the historical development. Enough: From day to day we saw the power of our oppressors change into powerlessness. All the more reason to fear that they would destroy us, too. On top of the rampart they were building in a circle barracks without windows to the outside. What did that mean? "You'll be surprised who will be put there," the commandant told our workers. Who else but we?! But to what purpose? The word "gassing" traveled from mouth to mouth like a specter of terror. We had heard talk about it, but nobody knew anything certain. Only much later did we discover that the gas had already been delivered, and that we, as though by a miracle, were saved by the Red Cross at the last minute. This uncertain fear, however, hung over our heads and did not let go of us for as much as an hour.

Nevertheless, even in the mica workshop one felt a gentler wind blow, which was welcomed with sighs and anxious doubts. A doctor dared to give me several days off because I was highly anemic. Out of gratitude I wrote him a short, light work in verse which turned out especially well, gave him pleasure, and attracted the attention of those around him, so that among his coworkers it became a kind of habit to have me write poems about them—a demanding task for me. But it was a rigorous training exercise for me to extricate out of the little that I knew about these people something worthwhile and to shape it into a concise but pleasing form.

All taken up by my thoughts, I ambled through the old alleys and courtyards to pick up my food. On these walks, which I stretched out on purpose, since I never was so alone and taken up with myself as then, I worked out my longer poems. Often I stood leaning against a tree, let my food get cold, captivated by a thought which stubbornly defied insertion into rhyme and the required meter. There originated my ballad "Tell me, friend, why, since we met..."

All my life I will remember the house with its old window-like eyes in front of which I paused abruptly, with an inner shout of joy. I had finally found the perfect setting for a strophe, whose clearness and smooth form I had polished so often. Now suddenly it had come to me, had lifted itself out of the labyrinth of my tangled thoughts. Finally it was perfect.

I had occasion to read my ballad to the much-honored Mrs. Aurednicek, who praised it highly. Musing, I went my way. Could it be that she was right? Or was it rash of me after all to believe in my poetic talent, a talent which should have come to the fore much earlier if it had been strong enough?

I gave a last recital in a small auditorium in the Magdeburger barracks. Then the Russians came. For days we had waited nervously, wondering who would liberate us, the Americans or the Russians. When the moment came at last, many prisoners—I among them—ran out onto the street which lead from Leitmeritz to Prague. Everything that separated us from this street and liberty had been trampled down by the prisoners by the time I arrived. Flags and signs welcomed the Russians, who slowly, in never-ending rows of tanks, passed us. Again and again prisoners broke the rows to offer their hands to the passing soldiers. In doing so, some were so carried away that there were several accidents during the course of the first few days.

An old Jew went back and forth in front of us and held us back: "Children, you successfully survived all those years, and now, when it's over, do you want to die like this?" The love the old man showed for us was so touching that he successfully kept us somewhat within the limits of reason.

Our whole life had been turned upside down. Suddenly we found ourselves at a different place of work; the mica workshop was closed! They gave us food, they helped us take care of the sick. In the time following this, we saw trucks arriving daily from other surrounding camps overloaded with deathly ill prisoners who found lodging and care in the large medical hospital within the barracks of Theresienstadt. Only now did we discover that there had been uncounted concentration camps in the surrounding area, of which Theresienstadt had been one of the largest, but by no means the most horrible. What these people reported surpassed our experience of suffering and horror by an inconceivable measure.

Moreover, Theresienstadt took on a new look. Even though we were quarantined because of typhoid, many prisoners knew how to steal through the barricades and go for long walks in the surrounding countryside. Some went all the way to Leitmeritz. The area had been abandoned by its inhabitants, many of whom had fled. The roaming prisoners therefore found houses devoid of people, horses without owners, empty shops. Some brought horses back to camp to let them graze on the rampart. Others sold what they found. The sight of a Polish Jew who probably always had been a peddler remains unforgettable for me. Barefoot he walked through the streets of Theresienstadt, laden beyond recognition with coarse boots, and offered them for sale.

These were nice, hot summer weeks. In the evening, when everything was quiet, we could hear the Russians, who still camped outside, singing their melancholy tunes.

I found work in the dietary kitchen, where I was finally able to get enough to eat—and to eat myself sick. What organism could tolerate such sudden change without harm! After I got well, I worked in the pharmacy, where I was happy and felt at home.

My boss, Anna Horpazká, was from Prague. She was a slender, pretty blonde and wore slacks. In more than three years she had become a tomboy, which was in total contrast to her kind, sensitive femininity. On the street, she always walked around with both her hands in her pockets and smoked, which now was allowed and even possible since with the arrival of the Russians tobacco was plentiful. She stood up for her workers—without being asked—with loyalty and energy, which earned her our highest respect. One could not help but try to fulfill her every wish. To her thinking, there was no difference between Czech and German Jews. Were we not all victims?

I had to—or better—I was allowed, among other things,

to clean the small attic room she shared with another woman. When I was done, I tried to straighten up the stuffed puppets which were lying on her bed, to prop them up and give them some expression. And so, one evening, when Mrs. Horpazká opened the door, they all sat there, offering her with their round hands made out of cloth a page with a poem written on it, expressing my gratitude better than a speech. Next day she admitted that she had cried with emotion.

At the end, we workers had even Germans working for us. Russians and Czechs had taken prisoners from the surrounding areas, National Socialists, but also, indiscriminately, harmless Germans, who lived in camp now and worked under our supervision. It gave me no pleasure, and among my acquaintances I found none who derived pleasure from giving orders to these people now. We took pains in our contact with them to be as objective and correct as possible.

Now at last we were able to climb up to the rampart during our noon break. Here I lay and listened to the trees rustle above me, and watched the clouds—freedom, freedom! Were we really free? Had our wish, whose impossibility we had almost accepted, now really come true? Up here, in my green isolation, a presentiment of the mercy of an unfettered existence slowly presented itself to me; here where I lived alone with myself in a precious solitude which life perhaps might not offer me again, there emerged once more in purified clearness pictures which had crystallized during these three years, and here originated a number of poems in which I compressed all I had experienced and seen. This high meadow where I liked to be in my shabby dress became like part of home to me until—when the quarantine was over—one city after the other sent vehicles to bring home the few of us still alive.

When at last it was Munich's turn, Mrs. Horpazká found another opportunity to stick up for me with her great, as it were, fatherly kindness. She went with me from authority to authority, from office to office, from desk to desk, to obtain some money for me for the next few weeks (a thought which would never have occurred to me alone). I followed her like a little dog. Of course, she got what she wanted.

Our leave-taking was short. "Mrs. Spies, you know that I like you very much. Write to me."

I wrote to her more than once, but never received a reply. My letters must have been caught by censors which are put up between nations even though people want to love each other. Finally, I stopped, because I was afraid it could do her harm. Whatever happened to Anna Horpazká?

We arrived in Munich on June 23, 1945; by the middle of August, the last Jews had left their place of undeserved exile.

What has happened to all those people whose help benefited me so much, who extended their hands to help me overcome?

My first supervisor, Otto Wolf from Brünn, one of the kindest, most cultivated men I ever knew, fell victim to one of the fall transports in 1944. Does he belong to the few who miraculously returned home? I do not know, and I would still give a great deal if someone could supply me with this information. The director of the Welfare Service Office: October 1944, to Auschwitz. Dr. Ruben, this splendid doctor, whose interest in humanity, whose beaming optimism could almost awaken the dead, who never found a way too long, never found an hour too late to look after me, to fight for another medication for me, who cared about the human development of his patients as much as their getting well physically, was sent to his death with a transport in March 1944 as the "accompanying doctor" of patients with neurosis. Mrs. Elsa, so magnificent and kind, and above all the others, my most important teacher, whose encouragement never tired even during times of extreme hunger in Theresienstadt, though she buried her beloved sister in this hellish place, she herself survived the horror miraculously, even though she gave us many anxious moments. We probably have to attribute her deliverance to the fact that she was allowed to live in the "House for Prominent People." She died July 12, 1949 in Hamburg, where she moved after the war. Kaff, the great pianist, whose performance gave us strength again and again to transcend ourselves and our misery, died in Auschwitz. Kurt Singer, whose music history talks let us forget time and place and ourselves, who was always available for everybody who needed him, became a victim of Theresienstadt. Philipp Manes, whose whole being in camp was devoted to our salvation through intellectual activity, was sent with his wife to Auschwitz. They ended there.

Poor Mrs. Mahler, who was not spared any suffering in life, and her paralyzed husband, both were devoured by Auschwitz. Friedländer, before whose forceful personality even death, one would have thought, should have bowed and stepped aside, perished in Auschwitz. Martha Geissmar and Herta Levi, my two friends who joyfully sacrificed in order to ease the life of others, also died the death of gassing. My Uncle Robert as well as six other relatives perished from deprivations and horrors in Theresienstadt. Dr. Jacobson is one of the few who survived. He was reunited with his family in England. Perner, the elder of our barrack, and his friend, Professor Blum, both did not return from Auschwitz. Dr. Alexander Gutfeld, who illustrated my "Mica Legend," survived despite his injuries and found new responsibilities in Berlin. Not so his wife (we had become friends), a well-educated Russian whose willingness to sacrifice saved his life, but in whose own mind the horrors of Theresienstadt left such sinister shadows that she ended her life herself more than a year after our liberation. Dr. Stiasni, the Czech physician, belongs to the few survivors, and so does Mrs. Aurednicek, but her son fell victim to the Nazi regime. She transformed this sorrow into superhuman greatness of soul.

Often, when the nights are long, or when I open myself to music, when the breath of spring obliterates the boundaries between here and there, when the first stars emerge in the evening sky, then I often feel as if all those who were so close to me did not die. Then it seems as if they still walk next to me, as if they touch my cheek. And it is especially my friend Martha who seems to search for me. I pass through these days like a stranger, and it seems as if a spirit puts the pen into my hand, so that the bridge between our world and the world of our dead will not collapse under the storms of our times.

Resonance

I feel so strange
Yet so melancholy;
When I was imprisoned,
I felt free.

Now, when the chain lies unused
On the floor,
I realize,
How heavy
Freedom weighs.

Certificate

MRS. GERTRUD SPIES.

For all your work which originated in Theresienstadt, we award you

honorable mention.

Your fine gift for composing vividly, your soul, which addresses that which is noble and good in humanity, even here behind walls, lost nothing of its purpose of striving for the highest, and forming into poetic works whatever day or night revealed to you.

To express warm recognition for all of this is the purpose of this page.

Theresienstadt, August 3, 1944.

Signed: Professor D. Erich Utitz
Free time Activity "Group Manes"
Signed: Philipp Manes

Diary. September 1944

September 16, 1944

One should live every moment as if it were eternal.
Twenty-six years ago yesterday my brother died on the western front. I woke up early, around five o'clock, at the time that the bullet hit him, and stayed awake until it was time to get up. Martha Geissmar accompanied me to the barricade by the south barracks. In the mica workshop again enormous noise and confusion. The three hundred women newly arrived from Holland had to be organized. I instructed my table of thirteen women how to split mica. The noon break was from twelve to twelve-thirty. First, standing in line at the food barrack. Then sitting on one of the benches up there on the hill, I ate, alone among many. They lay down on

127

the grass to sleep—people from all barracks, mostly women, all workers. They were lying around in the green meadow like dirty rags, a washed-out blue the dominant color. I climbed up and lay down in the soft, long grass under the acacia trees. They murmured among themselves above me, waved their green curtains back and forth, and let silver green light ripple down on me. I fell asleep and when I woke up I did not know where I was. There was shouting from the barracks because some women had returned a few minutes late. "If you do not obey orders, I'll show you!" etc. The afternoon slipped by with wretched dullness. The inspectors walked back and forth, hands behind their backs. The supervisor often was not around. The ladies at the table talked about their fates—carefully, still groping. Three hundred chattering women in one room! My headache increased. Here and there a man or a woman got up on a chair so as to be better heard and communicated something urgent to the general public. At five o'clock it is over. About a thousand people stream back to the ghetto through the small barricades. Good-bye, meadows! Until tomorrow! Then to pick up food in Building L 408. The soup is still hot. I sit down in the courtyard on a bench between old people and drink and ladle the soup to the end. Then back home to the west barrack. In the room, shouting as usual when all sixteen women are there. Rosi is hysterical again. Lately she puts a nightgown over her dress and sits around like that, perhaps to save her clothes. She yells and picks fights with everybody. The new one, a young woman from Berlin, who came with the transport from Holland, props herself up on the table and stares at her neighbor while she eats. I run outside, lie down in a small meadow by the canal—it is about six o'clock—and sleep for half an hour right into the yellow setting sun. Then back to the barracks again. I prepare my work for the next day. The noise cuts like knives into my mind. Dead tired. Rosenmann came with Liesel Steiner. He brought me some soup for the next morning. The three of us went up the bulwark, arms around each other. A soft wind fluttered above us. The day was dying. Stars appeared out of the growing darkness. We stood there and saw the last colors drown. On a faraway slope blossomed a cluster of gold flickering lights, a rare picture during war. We tried to guess its origin. "Why is there light? Where is it?"—"A quarter to nine, ladies and gentlemen. Please go home," the ghetto guard announced. Embedded in the hill of the bulwark is a small witch's house. It fell out of a fairy tale. From time to time, its door opened and closed noiselessly and light from the inside poured out in a golden stream over sand and meadow. Silhouettes walked in and out through this golden enchantment. Implements could be seen inside, hanging and standing up. Then the door closed again. It was quiet, very quiet. So quiet that we could hear the shadows walk. We went home.

Around two o'clock I awoke. Past the ladder which leads up to the bed on the second level, right in front of my face, through the open window I can see stars. My head aches, my nerves are frayed, pains in my right side. Images from yesterday start to talk to me.

My Years in Theresienstadt

Outside in the green terrain,
Where the wind gropes around the barracks,
A ghost sits there with a barrel organ
And plays and turns it without end.

Our ears have been deaf for a long time.
The organ always plays the same tune.
We always turn in the same circle.
Weary, the leaves fall from the trees.

September 17, 1944

The mica workshops are outside the ghetto, separated from it by a barricade and cut off from the world outside by barbed wire. There, on a large meadow, many dark barracks squat. Some of them are repair shops, but most of them are for production. The largest holds the mica workshop. Lately they have reopened it and eventually it is to expand to four shifts of 250 women each—a total of one thousand women. It takes up two barracks. Thursday, shift work starts—six o'clock until two o'clock, two o'clock until ten o'clock. Last week a large transport arrived from Holland. Three hundred women have already been absorbed. They have been given a supervisor who speaks Dutch. Yesterday, I was not quite as tired from work as on previous days. I went to visit Rosenmann around six o'clock. He helped me to exchange a can of condensed milk from my package from home for a four-pound loaf of black bread. Bread is more filling than milk. He filled my pot again with soup for today.

September 18, 1944

Yesterday morning by chance I arrived at work too early. This is advantageous since then I can take my time to do the preparatory work. I distribute knives, material, and small boards on which to cut, fight for the whetstone, etc, etc. The mica workshops were opened here in the summer of 1942; at that time they were still in barracks in the town center. I was brought in on August 7, 1942. On January 1, 1944, they were closed for a while, then reopened on September 7, 1944. In the beginning, the operation took about 150 to 200 women. Later, half of them were put on transports. There are about sixty to eighty left. Part of us, the old group, are detailed to distribute the material and to work at the scales, and some of us work at the inspection table to finish the split mica pieces, or to be the advance workers or group leaders, i.e., instructors. Right now I function as the latter. Our work consists of instructing, supervising, inspecting, and taking care of the workers. At times the discussion at our table is about love. Like a pretty play, my ears take in this light music. A friendly conversation, a luxury in these difficult times. It's a stupid detour for me to have to pick up my food in L 480. But since the south barracks are being provisioned from there, we, too, must have our little pots filled there. I am not too upset. The small courtyard, where the line forms, is surrounded by old walls, gates, alcoves, and small windows. Thousands of fantastic images appear in my foolish mind, and I am not in Theresienstadt any longer. When I arrived at Rosenmann's around 5:30 P.M., Liesel Steiner was already sitting next to him on the bed. She was wearing the white dress again, on which different-sized light and dark blue dots dance around like soap bubbles. Both were very excited. Wood chips were burning in their stove (they do not have wood). Only three of the twelve men quartered there were in and they were dozing. "We kept something warm for you!" And now came the food. Next day's soup portions were poured into the pots. We had cabbage—about a quarter of a liter—and water-based porridge, about half a mug. But then Rosenmann brought out something monstrous. It poured like blood out of the bottle into a real drinking glass—currant wine! Somebody had made him this splendid gift—it even contained a little alcohol. We three felt it right away and suddenly behaved like three boisterous children. I put my head on Rosenmann's big shoulder—as so often and gladly—and so we sat close to each other on the rough bed, using the low footstool as a table. I returned late to the world of my barracks, groping in the dark for No. 12 (that is the last of the five, where Herta Levi and Martha Geissmar live), pulling Martha out of the nocturnal darkness by the door. A short chat. In the room, a weak attempt at a festive mood—we wished each other well for the New Year. The word "peace" was used and abused. This morning—no, what am I saying—late last night, there were many disagreements again.

Diary. September 1944

Heaven is not satisfied with being blue only above us. It also comes out of small holes here in the meadow—right here in front of our work barracks. There are blue wildflowers blooming on bristly stalks. They look at me with their innocent eyes: "It's not our fault that we grow so wild here. We only want to see the sun. But we can't help being wild. It's too nice here." And that is the meadow, on which there is so much crying.

September 19, 1944

I have forgiven you!—I feel so easy—
All of you, whose arrows hit my heart!
I am a bird, no shot can reach me,
And yet open to the world and its beauty.

Thank you, thank you! I am so full of songs!
The autumn sun plays in my soul.
You pure forces of heaven, have you freed me
from myself? O culmination of ecstasy!

The barrack where I work now is the last one. A bit of grass—then the barbed wire. Behind it the "Aryan street." A wide field and another one, and then again an "Aryan street." There we can see the silhouettes of vehicles, bicyclists, and pedestrians, gliding back and forth far away, without hearing their clamor, like a picture in one's dreams, dark against silvery shining mountains as far away as heaven. They all move so easily, as a matter of course, as if freedom were nothing.

Yesterday, about a quarter after eleven, the twelve women from Holland stormed toward the exit of the barrack like a wild army; they wanted to be first to get their food. But they were stopped—and so they blocked the entrance and exit, clamoring loudly. Mr. Wolf, one of our supervisors—he used to be the main boss of the mica workshop (one of the nicest people I have met here)—had to work very hard to make himself heard above this storm. The horde had to return to their places until eleven thirty, and then the wild bunch was let out. Later on, Mr. Wolf, in his infinite kindness, almost apologized for them and explained the reason. Applause. After that, we got a gong to let all of us know what time it was. The gong is a blade from a circular saw and hangs from the beams. Next to it, on a piece of string, dangles a stick of wood—the hammer.

The way home passes by the Jewish ghetto guards, then the street rises past the Czech guardhouse, where gendarmes stand at the barricade in their green-gray uniforms (with cherry red), past the burial hall, which now is decorated with boxes of petunias. New, green-painted benches. Then over the bridge. To the right, the train tracks where transports come and transports go. Down there between the walls the setting sun is mirrored in the small blue canal. A few lucky ones work down there in their victory gardens. Cabbage and other vegetables excite desires in all who pass by. We keep going, past the hunting barrack at the Sokolowna, where our programs take place, where birch trees and willow trees sway in the wind, past the large fruit orchard on the left, where children lean on the fence and longingly look at pears or even try hitting them with stones. "Oh, please give us just one," they plead in German, Czech, Dutch, or Danish, when they see a man on the ladder, picking them. On we go, crossing the ditch. To the left, the food distribution. At the wall of the barrack the women line up, one behind the other with their pots in their hands. They are waiting for a new batch. In the evening, again a walk under the stars with Martha, arm in arm. We have to watch carefully, so as not to stumble over lovers, who are whispering in the shadows of the barracks. Everybody has to be home at nine P.M. But some jobs demand longer hours. Those people get passes from their place of work and are allowed to stay out longer with their sweethearts. The starry sky is magnificent. Here and there a goodbye kiss can be heard fluttering through the silence.

September 20, 1944

Yesterday—a free day. In the morning our room elder announces: "Please, go and pick up bread!" No one wants to go, suddenly everybody is busy. Threats, disputes, rudeness. Finally two women volunteer. They return half an hour later—now we have bread. Martha eats breakfast with me, sitting on my bed. The room is getting emptier and emptier—everybody goes to work. The door opens. A physician enters, a man from Berlin, in a white smock, behind him a nurse carrying a writing case and pencil. The physician is making his morning rounds. "Anybody reported sick? Everything all right?" He is gone in a flash.

After a while a knock. This is *his* knock! Quickly he enters. The mailman! We receive nobody with more loving attention than him. "When are you bringing me something?" "Why don't you bring *me* something?" "Why is there no word from home?" "Where is my little package?" He opens his bag—dead silence. Who will be lucky today? Suddenly he turns around, makes an innocent face: "Gertrud Spies—who is she?" Oh, he knows very well who she is! That's me! Is it possible? A package—and that on my free day! Quickly I offer him a piece of bread, with margarine and sugar! A delicacy! He accepts gratefully. I hurriedly get dressed and am off to the post office. After standing in line for a while at a counter, the form is handed over; it gets clipped and stamped at the next counter and is returned; it needs to be paid for according to size. Mine is a small package, a one-pounder, and it costs five ghetto crowns. A line at the distribution counter, I hand over the notice—and wait. A row of counters—behind them, taking up the whole room, are shelves with parcels, packages, and more packages. One post office for thirty thousand prisoners. Officials go back and forth, notices in their hands, looking for the packages according to number. At each counter sits a woman who calls out the recipient's name, watches the signature, and hands over the return receipt, with which the recipients are allowed to notify the sender of receipt of the package. Next to her stands an inspector, a Jewish official, who uses a knife to speed up the opening of packages and who inspects the content (Germans receive small packages, Czechs and Danes parcels). Finally, there is mine. I see it, I recognize the writing from home! From my Ruth! She's alive! She still breathes —there in the other world, on a different planet! The small package is inspected. Anything contraband, anything forbidden in it? Cigarettes? Coffee? Alcohol? Cocoa? Medicine? Newspapers? Letters? No. Nothing of the sort. He repacks it all, hands it over to me—I leave. Ruth's handwriting! The old address! And now the most important part: the date of the stamp! Hopefully, hopefully, I can make it out! Right, yes! With much effort I read: September 15, 1944. It took four days—only four days! That means, four days ago everything was all right at home, the house was still standing, she was healthy! What more can I ask for? I am happy. And now to the contents: cookies, noodles, some cubes of beef broth, and— a piece of sausage! Magnificent! Home. The noon meal is at Dr. Jacobson's with Martha. He lives in a tiny room on the second floor of a house in the back, darkened by a roofed-over balustrade along it. I contribute a beef broth cube. Martha cooks the soup. We all take our food, warm it up, improve it together, and feast. Chatter, teasing—soon all three of us are feeling a deadly fatigue. Across the couch sprawls, sleeps, and breathes with contagiously deep breaths the cousin of the "master of the house," Mr. Florsheim. Toward evening—to Rosenmann's. Liesel is there already mending her stockings. The three of us go up to the roof terrace. Here we eat our bread and sit together for a while, quietly. It is getting dark. A few more errands, then back to the barrack. I cannot see anything, but I know the way by heart. It caresses my feet.

September 21, 1944

Yesterday was filled with more contrasts than almost any other day I have experienced here. I don't know whether I am capable of describing it. Yesterday, suddenly shift work began, a day earlier than we had anticipated. I had the afternoon shift, from two until ten. I woke up early as usual. The beautiful weather drew me outside and I lay in the moat next to the narrow canal stream, which flows along so slowly between the meadows one sees almost no movement. The wind plays with the blue silken surface; algae and duckweed grow there. Tadpoles, water flies, and other such creatures jump, fly, and hop around, and above all of it, God's eternal silence, which sings of love and profound eternity. I had gotten hold of Keller's *Romeo und Julia*, and not being able to finish it due to the shortness of the loan period, enjoyed at least a few pages. Then I stretched out in the grass, let myself be embraced by the sun to its heart's content, and fell asleep. I woke up to the soft chiming of the tower clock, stretched a little, and enjoyed the silence, silence, and more silence. I shared the bread soup and dried vegetables with Schwabacher, who works across the way building barracks. Then I sat by the canal again. Shift at two o'clock. More than 300 lay on the ground between two barracks, and waited until they could go in. The morning shift had not yet left. We went in and tried to get ready. We tried. It was almost impossible in the tumult. The instruction that one person gave—shouting to be understood, i.e., to be heard—was countermanded by the next person or even by the first. This big reopening burst upon our bosses, taking their breath away. The horde was allowed to enter. Seeing these dead-tired faces, a person cannot understand where all this agitating chatter comes from. But young people are present, too, the age range is from eighteen to sixty. And not room for everyone. Long planks were brought in through the windows and tied to stools, creating benches, so all could sit. The barrack roared and trembled with this noise from hell. Too many had been called up—nobody knew where to put them. People, people, and more people. Calming words worked like balm on the confused and completely bewildered minds. People climbed onto stools, speeches were shouted through this ocean of noise. At last—silence. The boss, Mr. Kolm, spoke. He recited what we instructors now heard from him for the third time—every time newcomers arrived. Interesting that the speech had already been changed on the basis of two weeks' experience. It was less didactic, more down to earth, gentler above all, more humorous, and more humane. One had learned something. And now, after some organizational tasks, the instruction began. I related to people quickly. Suddenly, a pitifully wrenching scream—dead silence—everyone held their breath. At the next table a woman had a heart spasm. The doctor came, a nurse—a stretcher was brought in— medical orderlies carried her out. Next, a young girl at my table felt nauseous. She had to go outside several times and vomit. A young girl with feverish eyes—TB—tried in vain to leave work, to go home to bed. Finally, around six o'clock, she was allowed to visit the medical examiner. Go home at once. Unfit to work. Inconceivable, how she could have been brought here. A nice girl. An old woman is unable to split the mica. Stiff hands—each day she gets injections into her left hand. All this happens at my table with fifteen people. At six o'clock, food distribution. We take in some air. We lament, we despair. Then back inside again. We continue working, i.e., we clumsily and desperately attack the mica. Suddenly a general "Pst-pst." Dead silence prevails. A German visitor. A gigantic, handsome young person in SS uniform, accompanied by members of the Council of Elders who also make an appearance, walks through our room, says a few words, calmly, and leaves. The noise engulfs us again. Outside it is getting dark, the blackout curtains are pulled down. We section leaders are very busy. Suddenly we are told to work at the inspection table, to let everything else go. That's where the finished work is being checked, retouched, tested. The ability and calmness of the leader, Mrs. Lissy, was like a rock in the ocean. A warm feeling of belonging united us section leaders with new-felt affection. Suddenly we addressed each other with "*du*."* The last hour-and-a-half hardly any work was done at the tables. People squatted around with empty, glassy eyes. They were exhausted. At ten o'clock a column of three hundred people dragged itself home through the moonless darkness. Home?

---

*The personal or intimate address

September 22, 1944

Yesterday morning I found a slip of paper on my table—I was told to pick up my rations in the Hamburg barracks. This is a monthly allowance of sugar and margarine, given to workers who worked at least twenty-two days during the previous month. Anybody who has been ill for at least twelve days receives an illness allowance of sugar and margarine. Whoever has been ill for a shorter time, but too long to work twenty-two days, receives nothing. I went to the Hamburg Barracks—called C III for short—and picked up for myself fifty grams of sugar, thirty grams of margarine. I had been only an orderly last month. The amount depends on the type of work. Okay, fifty grams sugar, thirty grams margarine—I am happy with it. A visit to Dr. Jacobson, where Martha works as a secretary. Dr. J. is out. I meet Gutfeld on the street. He offers me his left hand—his right one was torn away by the war of 1914—his left one with which he can draw and paint so beautifully; we chat, he asked me to visit him soon, and he limps on—the war also had taken his left foot. In the workshop, hell is replaced by an orderliness approaching the military. Ten women leaders, twenty tables each with twelve ladies, six on each side. On each side of the wide middle aisle are ten tables placed perpendicular to the aisle. I have twenty-four ladies, table 5 and table 6 on the left. It is forbidden to leave the barrack during working hours; the seated workers are forbidden to stand around and to leave their place without good reason; it is forbidden to stay away, to stay in bed without doctor's permission, i.e., unless seriously ill, usually with fever. Each table *must* have twelve ladies. If one is missing, she *must* be replaced—thus, overstaffing. If there is one too many, she will have to be transferred or assigned to another shift. Each of the shift leaders, i.e., section or instruction leaders, is to take a written roll call; she has to collect food cards, etc. The late shift gets their evening soup or chicory coffee or cabbage at six o'clock and has twenty minutes to stand in line, eat, and rinse out their pots. When the weather is nice, we eat sitting in the meadow. The food for the early shift is put aside and can be picked up only at a quarter after two in L 408. This means we work from 6 A.M. till 2 P.M. with nothing to eat except two pieces of bread. That's all we can allow ourselves. Most of my women work pretty well. The young ones learn much faster than the older ones. The older ones are often stiff and ill. But there is almost uniform goodwill. I have mostly German women. To get the best possible results use friendliness; sternness achieves little. Eventually, two older women start to cry. Their nerves fail. Young girls only need a wink of the eye when something needs doing. It's done in a flash.

September 23, 1944

Yesterday morning, early on we were told: "By 8 A.M. everything will have to be polished flawlessly! Very high-level German visitors are expected." The early morning hours were spent polishing, cleaning, carrying water—beautification. By eight o'clock all clothing which usually lies around because of lack of space had vanished, mostly under the bed, and all torn and unpolished shoes (because of lack of shoe polish) were put away. Order and cleanliness to perfection. On one window there were "curtains," on another, none. A broken glass was replaced with a board. "German visitors" means inspection by the Germans. They had been announced before, but until now they have never entered our barrack. But one has to be prepared. You never know.

September 27, 1944

After many fainting spells and hysterical fits order has returned to the mica workshop. Only at starting time, at time of shift changes, and at the end is there still a lot of turmoil. On the twenty-third we had an aerial bombing. Nobody was allowed to leave the barrack. From far away we could hear the uncannily majestic noise of the American planes, but we were not allowed to go to the window. Then we could hear the dull roar of the hits, and somewhere the high noise of the defense. Slowly I experienced a tremendous feeling of the solemnity and power of providence. About one hour passed—then the long shriek of the all-clear siren. Change of shifts. Held back by the alarm, both shifts met coming and going, marching by each other, passing, as on the Corso—people and more people. Happy cheers—in the middle of the street stands a young fellow who plays guitar and sings. The clouded sky is clearing.

My Years in Theresienstadt

Another cloud approaches: Transport! Five thousand able-bodied young men are to be sent away. Schwabacher and Schneider are among them, too. The five thousand are divided into two parts, the first and the second transport. I accompany Schwabacher to the so-called sluice by the Hamburg barracks, I help push the cart with the baggage. It was

(Here my diary stops. This transport also went to death.)

Hunger

I get up during the night, I cannot lie down any longer. I am itching all over, the air is heavy, and the old woman across from me snores terribly loudly. I steal my way across the sleeping bodies, collide with them, whisper "sorry," and am outside. There is a line for the latrines. I hear groaning. I keep going.

Above the rooftops the moon dreams. He says: "Nothing is important any longer, not even death. You only think so." I ask him if he is the same one who shines at home. "Yes," he says, but I don't believe it. "Be quiet," he says. "Other things are more important."

"Don't you have a piece of bread for me? Or a potato?" someone asks. A little gray woman, transparent as a ghost, stands next to me. I don't know what to say. I still have some bread, but I am desperate for a slice. Suddenly, she moans, clutches her body, and leaves, bent over sickle-shaped like the moon in her light nightgown.

I had better go in again. The old woman has stopped snoring. Now my neighbor snores, the one who has breast cancer, who always lies half on top of me. If I sit back and snuggle up to the dirty little stove, I will not have to touch her.

Now it starts to bore away inside me. What the moon said occurs to me again: Nothing is important any longer. He is right, I tell myself, but saliva is gathering in my mouth, I can't help it. I want to get up again and go outside. "Quiet," begs someone who lies next to the door. I turn back.

The bugs are getting unbearable. My head aches. I don't want to eat, really. I firmly intend to keep my bread and to save it up. It's my hands' fault. Automatically they seize my bread bag and feel what is left. And what happens now happens by magnetism. I myself am not part of it.

The bread tastes bitter and moldy—they must have added chestnuts. I would have liked to cut my piece thinner, but it crumbles. Don't I have some meat? I think hard. Yes! Yesterday they distributed salt. I start looking for my salt. The paper rustles. "Quiet, quiet, quiet!" someone wails. I give up.

Outside, birds awake. One more hour before getting up. If it only were now! Finally I doze off.

I pick up my coffee on my way to work. It's half a liter of poisonous dark chicory brew, but it is still hot and goes through me. For a few minutes I am happy. Then the slave labor starts.

Break. Everybody starts eating. I can't. I have eaten my slice earlier last night. I close my eyes, so I do not have to watch. The others are quiet; they know. Again my mouth tightens. But my stomach is not responding any longer. Only a dry feeling, as if I had eaten tannic acid.

The work causes cold sweat. My fingers shake. Before my eyes things start to fade and my ears can't discriminate between noises any longer. Everything seems far away. Whatever my neighbor does happens on a different planet. I keep working.

Noon break. Bad-smelling, watery soup. We pour it out. Three middle-sized potatoes, two tablespoons of sauce. We eat slowly, with deliberation, to make it bring out the best. Potatoes with their skin on. We eat the skin, too.

I envy people who are capable of dipping their arms into the empty barrels to get at the leftover sauce on the sides. Their sleeves are thoroughly smeared when they reappear, but they got a little more. Why can't I do that? There is something inside of me that says no. Too bad.

In a corner of the courtyard, old people are digging through garbage with little sticks. They search. They are dispersed. They creep back. In the beginning I got sick watching this. But I don't feel anything any longer.

The old privy councillor talks to me: "How are you?" He even smiles. How can he have a smile on his face? It is all yellow and death has already put his mark on it. His eyes are bulging.

I am terrified. "What's the matter?" he asks me kindly. "Do I look so bad? Soon this business here will be finished for me." He points around him, nods, and leaves.

Going on, I pass a window which in times past had been a display window. Now people use it to store their trash behind it. But the pane still serves as a mirror.

My Years in Theresienstadt

Is that my face? Is that me? What does that in there have to do with me? But perhaps it's the other way around. Perhaps the image is the real one. The real one—the real one— I remember my conversation with the moon last night.

Again back to work. The hands slow down. Five-thirty. It's over for today. I know the way back in my sleep, but one has to be careful. The street is busy. Thousands are en route. In their hands they carry their small pot for soup and pick up their dinner. We must not collide. Shuffling skeletons are easily thrown down and once down, they do not get up again.

It's best to stay close to the wall. My knees are soft and weak; there is a weight on my back.

On my third of the mattress lies a slip of paper: A package from home can be picked up. I smile and sigh: it, too, has probably been ransacked.

At the post office counter, I have to wait. After an hour-and-a-half it is my turn. Yes, it is light and knocks when I shake it. It's from home. I look around me: no solitary space for me anywhere? I walk on and on and on. Finally at the rampart it is quieter. I start to climb. "Do not come up! Prohibited!" the guard shouts from above. I nod. I know. About halfway up I stop. Nobody sees me—I open it. It seems to have had a jar of marmalade, since the sides are still a little sticky. On the bottom some remains of porridge. A quarter of a loaf of bread —stone dry, and the apple which they left is partially rotten.

In my mind's eye the two small hands appear which put together this package for me. Perhaps they caressed this piece of bread, perhaps also an apple which is not there any more. And then they tied it up.

I sit down on a rock. I weep. Slowly my friend the moon rises. I go "home." At the food distribution they are standing in line waiting for fresh supplies. The line winds around itself. I see them from behind. The men have deep cavities from hunger where the head is chiseled from the neck; women's are covered by their hair. A few dead are carried past us.

The room falls upon me: "Was anything stolen?" I open it—they nod and fall silent. We ladle our soup. One woman comes up to me and gives me a potato. I embrace her.

"Tonight—a concert," one of them says. "Kaff plays Beethoven."

"Where?" I call out.

"Over there in the assembly room, where he always plays. All seats are taken."

"I'll try. Somehow I will get in. Or I will stand outside the door and listen to it from there." I run off, gasping. Hurry, hurry. I have to catch it.

The moon smiles down from the sky. Is this that other thing, the one that matters?

But tonight I will fight with myself again, whether to cut off an extremely thin piece of bread or whether to save it for breakfast. And I won't be able to sleep again, one night after the other, one year after the other, until—one way or another—there will be an end. And if I survive this, I will never again, in my whole life, complain about what those on the outside call deprivation.

Where To?

Night. Into the protecting harbor of dreams
All have slept themselves across.
But I lie here and cannot find rest.
Images move toward me,
Tips of wings touch the pillow—
Suddenly the door is ripped open!
Light burns the eyes. And all around
Heads raised—nobody sleeps any longer.
Deadly silence—no sound—no word.
Like a whip the tension breaks: Transport!
Narrow slips of paper with green stripes—
Who will be called?—Who will be caught!
Am I one of them—am I not one of them!?
—It's over—this time. There are three victims.
"Three from our room alone—
Then the transport will take more than a thousand."
"Into the dark? Into misery? Where is it going?"
"Will we see our children there?"
"Will it be even more terrifying than here?"
"Will they kill us?—What do we really know!"
Silence—no crying, no lamentation.
But someone whispers: "I knew it."

"I Heard It's Supposed to Be Auschwitz"

"**B**reak time," the shift leader announced. Automatically we put our hands under the table and pulled out our eating utensils; we got up, stretched our limbs, stiff from sitting, and rubbed our eyes burning from working in harsh, glaring lights. Then we stormed outside and stood in line. The evening soup was distributed. We stood and waited. All around us flat meadows and barracks, a lumberyard, and to the south the crematorium. A dark black column of smoke streamed again toward heaven. We sighed. Behind that, before our eyes, there was a lovely little town, painted like an unreal fulfillment of our dreams—Bauschowitz.

The line moved slowly, gliding forward. We could hear the muffled sound of the ladle hitting the barrel—dipping in, doling out, dipping in, doling out. It had a rhythm of its own.

The sun had completed its round above our misery. It stood in the west and from far away it threw a golden light over our meager world of barracks. The barbed wire sparkled. On the other side the Czech guard stood, leaning on his rifle, and watched us. His composure showed compassion.

We threw ourselves onto the grass and spooned our watery soup. We were done with it quickly. We had five more minutes. I stretched out in the grass and put my tired head next to some blue flowers, who like trusting eyes looked up into the sky. Free birds moved above us. I fell asleep immediately.

The gong struck terror in us. Again we were at work. The chatter of three hundred women engulfed me like an enormous wave. Suddenly it stopped. The supervisor had entered, stepped onto a footstool, and read us the latest orders. Starting tomorrow, we would be seated according to achievement. The higher the production up to now, the higher the demand from now on. Whoever could not handle it would be sent off with the next transport. Where to? We did not know. Just now another transport was being assembled. It was to leave early tomorrow morning.

"Did you hear, too," my neighbor asked, "it is to be the last transport for this year?"

"Maybe it is true."

"Maybe."

I get up.

"Where to?" asks the shift supervisor.

"To the latrines." She looks at her watch. "Be back in three minutes."

Outside, I let water run over my face, neck, and wrist, to

be able to keep on working. Fifteen minutes later I am fast asleep. My companions wake me. My neighbor starts a song, she is a professional singer. The young girls join: "In the evening, in the little town...." It is a happy song.

Suddenly everybody goes "Pst-pst." The team at the next table is a large tangle of people: An old lady has a heart spasm. Silence. One woman flies to the doctor. We open the window. The deep roar of airplanes cuts through the silence. The doctor arrives, feels her pulse, gives her medicine. The suffering woman gets seated by the window.

"Keep on working!" orders our shift supervisor. We grab our splitting knives. Slowly the wave of chatter swells up again. The shift supervisor approaches the ill woman: "You have to work again."

"I can't."

"Do you want to be part of the next transport?"

The dread opens the poor woman's eyes wide: "No, no, I'll try." She gropes for the working table. Again, I fight sleep. My hands work as fast as possible to banish it. Next to me they speak of transports, on the other side about Verdi, behind me about sports and the mountains at home, across from me about the fates of shattered families, about the Gestapo. It all mingles into a buzz. I sleep again. Somebody shakes me.

"Where do you want to go again?"

"To wash myself, so I don't fall asleep."

"Be back in two minutes."

As I return, they are singing again: "In the evening, in the little town...." The hours keep crawling along.

It is 10:15 in the evening. We leave the workshop. Our

feet, ice cold from sitting, welcome the movement; our backs fear it. Outside it is dark, we wade through mud. One woman loses her shoe—never to see it again. Up high the stars pour out their tears over us. The gun tower crouches alongside the black gate of the burial vault.

The road past the barracks has been closed because of tomorrow's transport. The freight train stands in the glaring stream of arc lights. People and more people, but in neat rows—the old ones staggering under the weight of their bundles, the sick ones on stretchers, the children silent and trembling. The Gestapo calls for them by number—into the train.

We make our detour. The alleys are quiet and empty; night curfew. Out of the dark muddy desert, the barracks we are housed in grow into the night sky like uncanny black animals. I enter the room on tiptoe, the wooden boots make such an annoying din.

"Pst, pst, don't turn on the light," a voice whispers.

"What happened? No lights allowed?"

"Yes, under penalty. In barrack No. 6 they still had the lights on five minutes after nine."

"Darn it." I sit down on my bunk bed. Next to me someone sighs. Above me somebody turns over. From across, a voice asks: "What's new?"

"There are not to be any more transports this year."

"I hope so. My boss has promised me today that I will never be sent away—he will protect me, he needs me," whispers Senta Joseph, "thank God."

"Yes, thank God," I answer knowing that somebody else will have to go in her place.

"How is Mrs. Mayer?"

"Poor. She moaned all day long. Now she's finally asleep. Be quiet, please. She always fantasizes about her children."

"What did the doctor say?"

"He shrugs his shoulders."

"Oh, dear."

I lie down to sleep. Some obnoxious thing crawls over my hand. I try hitting it. "Silence," someone says to me. But now I start to itch and burn everywhere. Nevertheless, I fall asleep. Tomorrow morning is shift change. That means: get up at half past four.

A glaring electric light wakes me up. So there is light after all! Two women are standing in the door, in their hands they have a pile of white slips with green stripes. I jump up, my heart pounds. Transport. After all. Am I part of it? Am I not part of it? Dead silence—they start calling. Mrs. Mayer moans in her corner.

"Helene Ring!"

"Here!" The slip is passed to her. "Start packing. Be ready by tomorrow night."

"Next. Luise Mayer."

A whisper: "She is deathly ill."

"Orders are orders. Be ready by tomorrow night."

"She cannot even stand up."

"Next. Senta Joseph ..."

"I!? But my boss told me ..."

"Child, what authority does your boss have? Tomorrow evening at seven by the sluice."

"What are we to do! We are not allowed to turn on the lights!"

I swing myself out of bed—I must help pack! We pack in the dark.

"I have to go to my husband!" Mrs. Ring laments. "I have to know if he is also part of it."

"You are not allowed to. You can't go out until after five."

"But I have to know."

We give up on packing, we can't see.

"How can I be ready by tomorrow evening!" Senta laments. Sobbing, she throws herself onto the pillow.

Mrs. Mayer wakes up. "What happened?" she asks gloomily.

"Nothing, nothing. Go back to sleep."

"When my Fritz returns...," she whispers and is gone again.

Half an hour later, we get permission to turn on the lights—in consideration of the order to pack. We start our work. The few belongings of the three women are pulled from below the beds and from the beds, and get mixed up. Mrs. Mayer turns and turns in her bed. We pack for her. The stars wane and flicker. The fresh morning air blows.

"I heard it's supposed to go to Auschwitz," my neighbor says.

"Auschwitz? Where is that?"

"I don't know. Not far from here."

"And what is supposed to be there? A work camp? A factory?"

"Will it be more terrifying than here?"

"Worse still! Certainly."

The door opens. Mrs. Ring falls into the arms of her husband. "I am also part of it," he lovingly says, "so we all go together."

"Where to?" He shrugs his shoulders.

Behind him, my girlfriend enters. On her pale features a bright smile. She approaches me, looks at me teasingly:

"Well—you have to stay—I get to travel."

I drop onto a bench. "Martha! You, too?"

Her dear mouth does not stop smiling, she strokes my hair from my forehead: "Will you help me pack?" she softly inquires.

"When I return. My shift changes today. I start work at a quarter to six."

"Then we have four hours together tonight. How nice."

Outside, the sun has risen triumphantly. "Joy, joy!" the birds exult. Mrs. Ring sits on the edge of her bed and cries in her husband's arms. Senta cries, too.

Carefully measuring, I cut off two thin pieces of my bread, throw them into my little bag, and get ready for work. Martha accompanies me to the guardhouse.

"Turn back, child, you are not allowed to stand here. Start packing."

Outside, in the workshop, it is as quiet as the grave. Overtired, tearful faces, anxious whispering. Many have not shown up; they were called up.

The high voice of the shift supervisor rips into the silence. "Ladies, start working. Now we must produce twice as much, since we have again lost part of our workforce." The ill woman from yesterday also has not come—she is packing.

My Years in Theresienstadt

"Today, some leave; in three days, some more," a voice sighs next to me. There, from outside, we can already hear the locomotive screaming, so shrill and mournful, as if it were crying the woe of a whole people toward heaven, as if to implore Him on high: "Help, help."

Slowly the wheels start moving. We hear the muffled murmur outside; we run to the window—

"Work, ladies, work!"

The shift supervisor has no more power over us. There, on the outside, the train passes, huffing and puffing—cattle car after cattle car—one after the other—no end in sight. There they go, our men, women, parents, children, brothers and sisters, friends—and the locomotive groans.

Under the roof of the cars small slots have been cut for airholes for the animals. Through these slots we can see hands waving and stretching. They know when they pass our workshop, they are sending us their farewells.

"Ladies, back to work! The inspectors are coming! The Gestapo is on the way!"

We fly to our seats, we grasp the knives and work feverishly. Growing more muffled and weaker, the rhythm of the moving train loses itself outside—moving out into the world!—toward the gas chambers of Auschwitz.

You Silent Stone

You silent stone, I groan to you
What no tear can say:
My heart has died inside me,
Never to cry or lament again.

I have become what you are,
Can neither love nor suffer,
Let the dark hours endlessly
Keep on passing over me.

At the Canal

Two walls lower themselves into the valley,
Two walls, steep and red,
And in the gorge, poor and narrow,
The Canal sleeps immobile—
All else is quiet and dead.

A meager meadow stingily emerges.
In the air, stiff with cold,
A choir of crows scatters darkly.
On the slope a silent dark gate—
It leads to the death vault.

In a Small Courtyard in the Back

The morning dawns, and a cool shadow surrounds the walls of the little courtyard in the back. With dawn a light wind comes up. The little tower, which rides on the old gray roof, bends down its slanted top and a sigh pierces the old yard. The wind gropes along the wooden joints, touches the pavement, and passes by the person who sleeps next to the fountain on a thin mattress, and blows away his blanket. The young man turns over, stretches his limbs, and opens his eyes. His gaze searches the fading stars in the sky. He breathes free and deeply: "How wonderful! I thank You, YOU! for this night! Alone—without others—without bugs—in pure air—and under your stars!" He folds his hands.

A gray apparition breaks out of the shadow of the wooden gallery. With dragging steps, in a dragging nightgown, bent over in pain, it steals toward a little wooden house. It opens the door—from inside a broad beam of light falls onto the pavement. It is the only light here. A rat jumps and smacks into the wall. The gray apparition lets out a howling scream.

Now another door is opened, but right away it is fastened. Is light a golden treasure which has to be kept inside? A man steps outside softly and walks toward the fountain. He lets his shirt slide to the ground and starts to wash his wasted body. He uses both hands and moves them as if they were holding soap. Then he dries himself with a cloth and hurries back into the house, softly, as he had appeared.

The gray of the sky turns into a light morning blue. Birds rise with soaring strokes. Others gather for a hopping rendezvous on the roof terrace. The cry of sparrows and the kiwitt of swallows and the intoxicated happiness of the blackbird all mix together for a concert. Suddenly a flutter—all are gone. A few women shuffling in badly fitting shoes come out of the house so loaded down with blankets, pillows, and mattresses that only their feet show. They spread the colored bedding on the ground, throw it over the ropes which stretch from wall to wall, and start to search, to brush, to beat. One woman brings an umbrella, she opens it—it is raining brown spots. She throws the umbrella away; all cry out; the women take off, then return with a bucket of water and put the umbrella into it. An old woman starts to mop the stairs, the yard.

The colors have taken on the sober energy of the day. The beds shine colorfully against the deep blue, radiant sky.

Two white shapes come out of a door. They carry a stretcher. Next to them a nurse in her uniform. "Hopeless," she whispers into the ear of one of the bearers. The terror-stricken eyes of the dying one look at her. The dying ears seem to have heard it. The shape under the blanket cannot be made out any more, it has wasted away. It has become a part of the stretcher. The nurse steps up to it, pulls the wrist from underneath the blanket, the small almost invisible wrist, and starts to pull on it. She pulls back and forth, but the watch will not come loose. The sick woman does not move any longer, but her eyes, her black holes still show life, terror, and are alive enough. Finally, the nurse lets go of the sick one's hand, like letting a dust-cloth fall, or a piece of empty paper. The bearers carry the stretcher away.

They collide with a giant, who wears nothing but a long, wide pair of pants on his copper-brown body. He carries mattresses into the yard, dirty, old, worn-out mattresses, goes away and comes back with a second load and a third one. The mountain gets higher. He pulls out a bunch of wood shavings, puts a match to it—the mountain starts to burn. Stench and smoke spread. A wrinkled old woman screams out of a window: "Yes! Cook them. Damned pests. Don't let even one escape!"

A little woman wearing a head scarf totters past: "Oh God, my beautiful mattress! What will I do now?"

A back door opens. Slowly, with measured steps, two women appear and lead a sick person between them, who painfully, shakily puts one foot before the other. They take her to the bench by the sunny wall; she collapses, sinks slackly into herself.

"But this smoke, these fumes! She cannot breathe here!" "Not inside because of all those people, not outside because of the fumes. Well, what can we do?" They sigh and walk away. The sick woman puts her back to the wall and closes her eyes.

"Not so fast, not so fast. I cannot keep up." Four shaky old men carry a dead one. Do they carry him? No, they pull him, drag him through the dust, he is too heavy for them. Their own almost dead bodies are supposed to carry a dead person! They go to the shaky outside stairs on the wall of the house. They disappear with their load into a dark room.

A young woman carries a pitcher with water across the yard. The smoldering pyre causes her to cough. She covers her eyes. She kneels down by the stairs and lovingly caresses a few delicate flowers blooming unconcernedly in the daylight among the shards. "You are so lucky!" She lifts her pitcher, waters her loved ones, and walks on. The four old men loudly rumble down the stairs. This time without the dead one.

"Ten o'clock. Take the bedding inside!" The scream comes from one of the windows. The house elder. From all the doors, across the roof gardens and galleries there is running and patter—the aired-out bedding disappears. The yard is gray again. The last ones are about to turn toward the house, when suddenly, everybody stops still—the air freezes, the birds whir away. Black shapes, flashing buttons. Heavy boots hit the pavement. Fat women in uniforms march up in rigid lockstep.

"The house elder! Where is the house elder?" An old man with a shaved head and rounded back hastily rushes out of the door, and stands bowed and tense, as well as he can, the wasted old man before young giants.

"Open up. We want to see what they have hoarded here." "Step outside!" cries the house elder. "Everybody out of the room! The sick ones, too. Inspection, house search! Leave your purses inside! Only people outside!"

Like a swarm of bees, women stream through a narrow door. They stagger and reel as if they were night-blind. The uniforms disappear into the cavelike doorways. The scared group gathers under a projecting roof. They only whisper. They stand motionless, and yet a shiver runs through the little group.

The whole house is engulfed in silence—frozen, death-like. From the barrack yard the rolling and turning over of barrels and troughs can be heard. After some time, the door opens. Hiding their harvest in their bags, the uniformed women step outside and turn toward the next door.

"All men outside! Take nothing with you! Leave every-thing!"

While the women silently file back into their dark, cave-like door, the men on the other side stream out of theirs. The same silence—until suddenly the door springs open, a per-son steps out, holding a white little stick up high: "To whom does the cigarette belong? Who smokes here?"

Silence. It is so quiet, so full of foreboding tension, that breathing can be heard and the flapping of a crow's wings, fluttering from one roof to the other.

"Well?" the young giant asks.

Silence.

"Okay. Please yourselves. All of you will be put away."

Then a man steps out of the throng—young, tall, thin, his closed fists shake. He does not say anything, he only stands there. "Where did you get it?" The young man is silent. Then the other one lifts his arm: "Ghetto guard! Take this man away!"

A fist comes down, blood flows. The black shapes leave the small, walled-in, silent square, their steps fade away, become fainter in the distance. Two, wearing black-gold caps, lead between them something swaying, bleeding. A tense whisper flutters after them:

"He won't come back."

It has turned quiet now, even more so than before. Slowly and bent over, tired, thin women with buckets and pitchers drag themselves down the stairs and form a chain one after the other, in a corner of the yard. "Maybe there is a little trickle here. There is nothing left anywhere in the house." They open up the spout, a meager silver stream dawdles down. They hold their containers and slowly, very slowly, they fill up. The women step impatiently, from one foot to the other, disputes boil over, start to spread—until it all crumbles away by itself.

A woman has entered the yard. She throws her bucket far away from herself and suddenly—has she lost her senses?—stumbles without seeing or hearing over a sick person warming himself in the sun, and, numbly—yes, surely without feeling anything!—beats her head again and again against the wall. "My child! My child! It's not true! My child! No! It is not dead! It's not true! My child! My pride! My only consolation!" And she hits her eyes with both her fists, and a long, hollow groan emanates from her breast. The gray bent-over skeletons of the water bearers surround her, cling to her, embrace her, try to console her.

"My child. Give me back my child! It can't be true! It's not really true!" Her voice has taken on a pitiful, imploring tone and changes into a monotone, sobbing, only to suddenly start to howl again:

"No! My child is *not* dead. No, no. It's not true. It can't be true!" And her hands clutch the damp, cold wall, groping back and forth as if she were searching for something. She howls and searches and screams as from a knife thrust and at last she collapses like a rag.

They carry her away. "The child died from typhus," somebody explains softly as she disappears.

Young women in slacks arrive, food bags slung over their shoulders as if on a field trip, self-confidently marching like men. They clean their eating utensils under the thin stream of water. On the rooftops and balconies old people stretch out for their noonday nap, small, wrinkled, pale, washed-out rags. Two children sit down on the edge of the fountain. They take out a primer and start writing. But an old man, a little black cap on his white head, limps over with a cane: "Put away your pads, you two. You know that learning is not allowed! Haven't we had enough misfortune here today?" The children look around and flee into the house.

A fat, tall woman with tinted hair, her hands in her pants pockets, music notes under her arm, opens the door to a small room. No, not to the room where the dead man moved in—it is the room next to it. A young man follows her. We hear a chord, piano sounds ripple, a deep, powerful woman's voice practices scales—up and down, up and down—the piano keeps up with her. She practices, one must not relax. Perhaps, perhaps.... Now she climbs up high, turns shrill.

The sun has reached its zenith. Tired, the birds are silent. No clouds in the sky, dusty flickering fills the air. Two men bend over the wooden railing of the outer stairs. One sucks on an empty pipe. They talk. "I saw it, he got a double portion. He can't deny it."

"It's okay by me. Yes, I don't care. Listen, do I feel better, you or I, if he gets less? It's okay by me if he has enough to eat. I am unhappy no matter what, and so are we all. At least *one* of us has enough."

"That's right. Now even you defend this bum. We should accept that our food..."

"Be quiet. You cannot change anything, this is how it is everywhere when there is hunger. Haven't you been lucky? Haven't you known a cook personally?"

"Me? No! And if—I would not accept anything—not a thing!"

"Come on, don't be foolish, everybody takes advantage of an opportunity."

"What are you saying? Did you ever see me..."

Their grating voices cut through the air. "Quiet!" someone yells from the other side. They lift their gray heads. There, on the other side—oh yes, over there—the dead man is taken away. The four old men are doing it again. They look so wasted in their shabby clothes. They cannot carry him, so they drag him. They drag the body by the feet downstairs, the back of the head hits each step—"bump—bump—bump —bump." They have reached bottom.

The five disappear into the gate. Passing them a young woman rushes toward the fountain. She collapses by the rim, buries her head in her hands, her hair falls forward, covers her eyes and ears. Sitting, she sways back and forth, groaning. "I cannot go on, I cannot go on!" Suddenly she starts sobbing. "I cannot listen to their voices any longer, I cannot watch them eat! I cannot—oh dear God, I cannot watch any longer, how they sit and stare ahead and think about their hunger! These wasted skeletons! I cannot watch any longer, when they undress—how they exchange recipes with greedy eyes—how they write them down! When they cannot even spare one potato! And then they start to quarrel! I cannot listen to it any more. I cannot bear it!" She stops up her ears, she falls silent. And then it starts again: "Oh, take me away from here! I don't care where you send me—physical labor—even more hunger! Only let me see no more old people. Only away, away!" Again she holds her head in both her hands, as if she could silence the motor inside her head. Only her shoulders are still moving and little wet pearls fall into her lap.

But then she jumps up. A dried-up, red-eyed old woman sits down next to her. "Couldn't you hold the wool for me?" And she works on winding her skein which she kept under her apron. The young one puts the wool over her wrists and stands totally still, as if nothing had happened.

"Yes, I also cry often," the small apparition of hunger says. "They killed my son; they sent away my daughter, I don't know where to. I am all alone here—and always hungry, always hungry."

"Wait!" exclaims the younger one. "I have two potatoes upstairs!"

"Oh, you good person! You good person!"

The young one hurries into the house. Strange, she thinks, that old people complain about hunger a lot more than we do. And they have nothing to do ... perhaps that's the reason?

The old woman is left all alone in the yard. The sun is scorching.

Carefully lurking she peers in every direction—then she lifts up her trembling body and limps away, bent over and stiff, toward the compost heap piled up in front of the wall, picks up a small stick and starts to rummage. She has barely started when a door opens and like gray rats, another one creeps out—and a third one from another door. They rummage, they rummage, they are looking for thick potato peelings. "Hardly any potatoes today. Why did they peel them so thin?"

"Get away! I will drive you away!" somebody calls from the roof garden. "Do you all want to croak of typhus?" The house elder! They shrink away like rubber and hide their finds in their bent laps. Then they slip away like sparrows.

"Come, come, sit down with me, I have something good for you!" A man, a woman. They sit down whispering. "Drink, drink!" They unwrap a pot. "Pure beef broth, good hot beef broth!" The liquid, clear as water, glistens in the sun. They drink.

Slowly the shadow of the wall grows right into the middle of the yard. The yard fills up with returning workers, men and women. They sit around, wherever they can find a small place. The old men come out of their smelly rooms, turn their faces east, and start to pray. Silence descends everywhere, only their monotonous murmuring hangs in the air like a thick cloud. Children flit past, and old women. They sit around idly and brood. The day pales and tires, a chill spreads. Slowly one after the other gets up, goes away with an empty pot, and shortly returns with it—barely filled. They eat, they wash their pots, when all of a sudden a feverish undertaking starts all around them. A few crude benches are dragged in, a platform is built. In the gate a sign is planted:

Evening entertainment!

Cabaret!

A lecture with music!

In less than half an hour, the narrow square is overcrowded with people. The older ones sit on benches up in front, the others stand close together, head to head, shoulder to shoulder. Hundreds of tall and short people, young and old, men and women. And then all hell breaks loose up there. One person plays the accordion, contorts his limbs, makes faces. A pretty woman bellows melancholy eastern songs into the evening. A young man tells jokes. An older one makes a speech, makes everybody laugh. A couple, pink with make-up, comes out; the young man sings soprano, the woman sings tenor—everybody screams with pleasure. In the midst of it a gloomy silence: An old man reaches out, his throat rattles, he turns his eyes up and falls to the ground. He is taken away. "This is not for old people. They cannot take the hunger." Somebody made the remark. And the show goes on.

It is evening now. Lonely, the lantern of the moon sways above rooftop and yard. Somewhere a harmonica laments.

The last lights are extinguished. Stars shine above the roof-tops. "Good night"—two people clasp hands, shivering. Then each hurries away in his own direction. On the roof terrace a silhouette of a young man rises against the sky. A door opens, something bright, floating, flies into his arms. They spread a blanket. Now one cannot see them any longer, they have melted into one.

"I must go back in, my mother is waiting."

"You stay with me. Who knows, in three days I may not be here any longer, perhaps we both won't be alive any more." He pulls her head toward him and puts his living chain around her.

Down below, the door to the little house opens, closes, opens, closes. Light, darkness, light, darkness. Always bent over, a figure waits in front of the door, supplants the one coming out and is itself supplanted by the next one coming out of the darkness. An open roof window flaps in the wind. A shadowy being climbs out and hangs his legs over the rooftop. Sitting there, under the eye of the moon, the young person opens up a bright piece of paper and, with eyes bent closely over it, concentrating, he starts writing. Then he looks up into the sky again, then he continues to write. His lips are whispering his thoughts. Above these last human beings uncounted stars meditate far away and solemnly—witnesses of eternity. The old walls sink back into the shadows.

Again one day closer to the end. What kind of end?

The wind howls,
The rain trickles down on
Roof and planks.
Oh, tell me, my child,
Where will I find you!
When will we meet again!

The world is large,
And into the lap
Of the earth we are pulled.
You are poor and naked,
You have no home—
You won't see your child again.

Fate tore at my dress:
"Give it to me!"
Naked I stood there in the storm of time
And empty.

"Give me your heart and make me full!
Ah, what ecstasy."
It drank my blood, and my breast
Became dead tired.

I sank down and would not
Have awakened—
Then the spirit's light of the spheres
Pierced through my night.

The Little Tree

For a long time, no mail from home. One day passed like the next. The world had drawn a circle of silence around our camp, and here we sat and held our breath: Must we forever be afraid or was there hope for us?

The weather had turned cold after all, starry cold, after the almost inexhaustible rain of the late fall. The yellow clay earth, so giving and fruitful in summer, soft as quicksand in rain, was frozen into small crinkly waves and glittered maliciously.

There was no more stealing potatoes at night. The moonlit nights were too bright, and though the cars were still standing on the tracks, they had been emptied long ago, and the potatoes were stacked in basements. Train tracks went straight down the middle of the main street and it was a strange sight to see freight cars strung out between the low, old houses for months at a time. Some passenger cars were at the head of the train. Once, during an unguarded moment, I stole into one of these cars. It was like in bygone times, sliding doors, curtains, seats, windows to look out—I made certain that not a soul was around. Then I sat down, closed my eyes, and said to myself: I am going. I am going home. Just as if I were still alive. But I was already dead.

If one walked past the cars and kept on walking, one would leave town. Day after day we had to go this way; it led to the mica workshop. We walked this way by night and returned by day—or in reverse depending on the shift. On the bridge over the moat, the shifts would meet and nod a weary hello.

On the outside, close to the road, stood a little house where Czech gendarmes stood guard. Sometimes we could see them standing by the door, often they only looked out of the window and watched us. They had to make sure that nobody would take to the road. Here, on the outside, it was actually only the barbed wire—and our fear—which separated us from the world. Often we played with the thought. But we kept it at that. The foreign country we would have to cross, the foreign language, those we left behind who would have to suffer for us—and after all, the gendarmes had rifles and were accountable for us.

Around Christmas time I was working the late shift and Christmas Eve was an evening like any other for us prisoners. We sat under our hanging lamps, twelve each, grouped according to performance, and split the mica—a mixed bunch we were, all stamped by the same fate, with the same ancestry, yet from three different countries, of three different confessions. Some of the young girls started to sing Christmas songs, others joined. But the mica had to be split quickly. They became silent soon and it grew quiet, we had had a long day. The split mica was put in boxes and sparkled like soap bubbles—or Christmas tree decorations?

"Stop working," our supervisor yelled. It was ten o'clock in the evening. We cleaned up, cleaned the tables and floor, and went outside. Before us mountains of coal stretched into the night sky, beneath us the earth burst.

"We probably will never experience a real Christmas again, like we had at home," I heard somebody next to me say. And my answer: "Why should we. I only wish for an end. Even if it were down there."

The dark troop of women workers walked almost noiselessly up the hill. To our right stood the acacia trees, naked and huge. We wound our way toward the bridge. The sky sparkled with stars. It smelled like earth, like open spaces—it smelled like freedom. Before our eyes stretched the wavy Bohemian flatland up to the embracing foothills. Tired and hungry for bed we passed the little guardhouse. The trees on the way looked like stony apparitions.

But what was that? Had stars fallen from the sky? The little guardhouse was surrounded by darkness. No sound could be heard. The gendarmes had retreated. We could see no one. After all, they weren't allowed to speak with us. And it was night. And it wasn't necessary that they should talk to us. Because in front of the house, rammed into the earth, its head full of lights and stars, stood a lovely little tree. It stood there, alone and quiet, and it smiled at us, trustingly, like an innocent child in a strange, cold world. The lonely men inside had decorated the tree for us, probably with awkward fingers, and had put it up for us, outside, against the background of a wide, homeless, dark, winter night. There was no difference then between Protestants, Jews, and Catholics. The tree was to give light to all of us, forbidden and in silence—on the path, into our hearts, despite all the dangers to which love is exposed and to which those who practice it, where force rules, are exposed.

This happened many years ago. The little tree not only gave us light, but it warmed us, too. And some small amount of the courage of love by those who had put it up and had decorated it with lights still illuminates and warms us today—those few of us who were allowed to stay here—for a short time.

Selection

The camp seethes and bubbles in feverish excitement: Again they are registering the "privileged ones," fathers and mothers of the so-called half-Aryan children, who had to be left at home. There is a long line in front of the commandant's office and every one of us knows that it is about life or death, that inside there are two SS officers, next to them two secretaries, and every one of us will be questioned by them. Then—and we know that, too—the slip of paper with all our statements will fly carefully aimed through the air. If it flies to typewriter Number 1, it means: Transport— nobody knows where to. But that it means the end, that we all know. They have threatened us with this transport for a long time. If, however, the slip of paper flies from the hand of the officer to typewriter Number 2, then we are—for the time being!—saved. And to think further than past the next corner, nobody dares. Slowly the line moves. Half a day has already passed. And we still are capable of feeling fear, after years of imprisonment!

Now it's my turn. There they sit, the two of them, behind one table, and to the left, the secretaries at their typewriters. The first officer is Austrian, handsome, friendly—oh, if only I...But my turn is with the one on the right. He is short and terribly cross-eyed.

This much I know: It all depends on our type of work here in camp—and on our children. Especially, sons can be of use, if they are employed in war-related or some other work considered essential. But my son is ill....

"Well, what about you? Do you still work?"

I answer him.

"And your children? A son?"

My heart pounds. A sick son—how can he save me?

"Well!?" He is getting impatient. His cross-eye looks at— I don't know what....

Should I lie? I do not dare. Who knows what they have written down. They know more about us than we do. And should he find out, I would be lost. I will tell him about my daughter. "My daughter..."

"Your son! What kind of work does your son do?"

"I—my son is ill."

"Well, that will pass. So what..."

"No, it will not pass....He is in an institution ..."

"Well, he works there!"

"No, he can't do anything, he is too sick."

"What do you mean too sick! There is work to do every-where, even in institutions. Well, what does he do there?"

I start perspiring. "I don't know, I...the others..."

"I am not interested in the others, listen to me! I want to know what your son does! So, think about it."

"I, I..." My heart pumps desperately. "I don't know..."

"Oh, yes," he yells at me, "you know perfectly well. Now let's hear it."

He looks at me, I look at him—one of his eyes looks away from me, the other is pointed at me. For a moment, I think there are two people here who speak to me at the same time. At last, it dawns on me: I am supposed to lie! Of course! He is putting the words into my mouth! He wants me to reach for the liberating, the life-saving lie.

"In the garden," I stutter. "They have to work in the garden..."

"So it is garden work." His eye looks off into infinity and the slip of paper...flies to typewriter Number 2.

I don't know how I got outside.

And that instead of me someone else would have to go, since they have to fulfill a certain quota, too—I only thought of that hours later.

Did *he* think of that in that minute—who can tell....

The Journey Home

I slept and was content. I had given up thinking and grumbling and lived without self-determination. All my strength for suffering had been worn off due to the persistence of my misfortune. I wanted nothing—because I was nothing. It had taken a long time until I was at that point and it was more than I had dared to hope.

And then, on a late summer evening—the Russians had been there a long time—someone woke me up, shook me, and yelled in my ear: "Munich is here!"

"What?" I asked, although I knew what it meant. Munich finally also had sent a vehicle or two, to pick up those few of us who had survived. Munich ... the picture, which had kept alive our desires and with it had kept us alive, now emerged, indefinite, pale, and far away like a dead vision, and wore false laurels. Munich—had lost its meaning.

"Let me sleep." And I turned over on my bag of straw and wrapped a blanket around me. But sleep did not come. Angrily I brooded during the short night and with the first blackbird I pulled myself up.

All the time I had grumbled: almost all cities had already sent their vehicles. A few days ago, it had been Frankfurt. Only from Berlin, Hamburg, and Munich there was no sign. Well, good, now it was time. And it did not hurt and did no harm—I was dead.

Stepping out, I sniffed the morning air. Whoever has ever been imprisoned knows what a feeling of happiness the wide sky radiates. I went to look for Munich.

Naturally, Munich was Munich—for three years I had boasted about it. Munich would send the best-looking vehicles. I did not find them. No bus anywhere in sight, no company car. She must have been dreaming last night? I sat down on a turned-over wooden barrel and absentmindedly I noticed an old truck, which I had passed several times. Unconcerned, my gaze fixed on its back. I had read its number a few times backward and forward. Suddenly, I jumped up: Munich!

What—they sent such a wreck!? Was that all they could do for us? Not enough that they had cast us out! What did we know of the extent of the destruction at home—Munich was Munich and had to send nice vehicles. What would the others say, when they saw—that!

But then the preparations started. I went to the central drugstore and told them that as of today I would no longer come to work. Standing in the door, my boss—a pretty blonde woman from Prague—looked at me: "Ah, did Munich come?" She embraced me, and we cried together.

I made the rounds to all the offices. And in between I packed my few belongings. I did not want to take my two towels, but my boss said: "Take everything, there is much poverty in your homeland." She knew better than I; the Czechs had kept in touch with their gendarmes. She mixed a moisturizer for me and gave me a bag of sugar for the way home. Oh, the sugar. I had no idea then that I had a tiny granddaughter waiting at home who had hardly seen sugar since she was born.

It took a few more days before I left—actually I should not have gone with them at all, because of the quarantine. Two weeks ago I had found a pair of lice at the bottom of my shirt. Incubation time is three weeks. But I had killed the two and had not told anybody about them. Who says that they had bitten a sick person?

Actually, they had not. But I did not know that then.

And then, the morning came. The sun was still sleeping, but I ran out. All through the long, warm summer night I had heard a lot of noise and shouting and when I got there I found out why: All the others had fought for their places, they had stayed awake all night. No more room for me. There I stood with another companion and a very old married couple. There simply was no room for the four of us. The yelling continued on the truck while they were loading up the little trailer with backpacks and shifting suitcases. My acquaintance started to cry. That's when somebody put a ladder to the trailer, pushed me, then the couple, and then Irma

—they took away the ladder, I felt a jolt, those left behind waved and the ones from Berlin shouted: "Have a good trip! Goodbye!" I did not know how I felt. I was on my way.

To leave Theresienstadt—my dream for three years, a dream of an eternity! How did it happen that a dream stopped being a dream? But in reality, we left ourselves behind, in an almost inconceivable hurry we distanced ourselves from the world into which fate had thrust us, a world to whose terrors and sufferings habit shackled us.

Turrets and ditches dissolved like images which had lost their power. Barricades and barbed wire—none of it real any longer. Day dawned around us—a strange world, a world much, much too large—how would we still fit into it?

During the trip the suitcases started to slip. They slipped toward us from all sides. The sun burned down on our bare heads. The little square space we occupied grew smaller and smaller, as impossible as it seemed. We stepped on each other's toes, tried to avoid it, and hurt ourselves when hitting the suitcases—eventually, there was no giving way. A bug slowly walked across the blouse of the old lady.

Prague. I had never seen it. We raced through. Streets like all other streets in the world. A streetcar! A real streetcar! And people sat and read newspapers as in long bygone days. We kept going.

And then the truck stopped on the open road. Everybody off! It was the first stop. After all, you have to get off sometime on a trip.

O dear heaven, incredible! To the right of the street verdant forest beckoned!

Had there existed forests all these past years? The trees swayed in the morning wind and played with the leaves; golden spots and stripes trembled on bushes. Strawberries, delicious! They let themselves be picked—we ate them, made little bunches. And on we went. And the suitcases kept slipping, branches hit our foreheads and eyes and left their marks. It did not matter . . .

Barricades. The Russians were very exact. They counted us, collected our passports; the leader of our transport had to bargain with them; it took a long time; the sun was burning.

And then the Americans. They thought it was funny, they let us hold our passports up, nodded, and laughed—keep going!

Late in the evening we arrived in Neustadt on the Wald-naab. Above the mountainous little town floated the moon, mysteriously silent. Someone played a harmonica. A tepid wind blew from the mountains. A castle lorded it over the crooked-gabled houses—or was it a ruin? I cannot remember. In the moonshine, the cobbled pavement seemed like mountains and valleys. Somewhere water was rushing. It was like a fairy tale.

When I think back now, this night still appears to be the most wonderful one of my life. I discovered that the world had not died. Life went on, and it went on inside of me. The thread had not been cut.

Americans lifted us out of the truck, they gave us food,

we were honored guests of the city. Indeed, we even sat at tables and carefully showed each other that we had not forgotten how to behave in company.

The straw was fresh and clean, the floor on which it was spread, polished. We slept deeply and undisturbed by bugs. Next morning—it was a Sunday—I went down to the small river. Bells were ringing—such a long time since I had heard any! A farmer's wife, dressed in peasant dress, passed me, slowly, solemnly, without hurry or fear; she did not turn to look at me, though she must have known—she walked on.

Then they told us to take off the yellow Jewish star. Why, I thought? (I had learned to look at it as a medal of distinction.) Now even we latecomers were given a place to sit. We got into the truck. Today it's all the way to Munich! The sun burned mercilessly; my moisturizer made the rounds.

There were a few among us who had left Munich only four months ago. One woman assured me that my apartment had still been standing then. It was all the same to me. Apartment, no apartment—how ridiculous! What was wrong with people that they cared about things like that.

Old cities, destroyed train stations, endless highways—a glowing sunset—Munich!

What was that? Rubble, debris, ruins! Certainly, one had heard all sorts of things. But that it would look like this?... And that it could happen to me! And that perhaps I did care after all? What did Munich have to do with me? After all, had I not—with a calm heart—reckoned on never seeing it again? And now...

A bunker? What? New to me. And here—my heart

pounded like a storm: ruins, ruins—Ungerer Street! Or perhaps this was not it? Freilitzsch Square, more hideous than ever imagined. Here, friends had lived, here.... But it already lay behind us. We sped down the empty, ruler-straight Kaulbach Street. Deep down in their trench, people stirred. Suddenly I noticed that I had jumped up. "They are waving," I shouted. "They are waving."

That was the signal. Now everyone jumped up from their seats. The paralyzing terror left us, we waved back—closer, closer—the truck stopped. It was all so confusing, so incomprehensible. People surrounded us.

Again ladders were put up. Laughing and crying they embraced each other, those from below with those from above. I was helped down gently. There they were in each other's arms, the others. I looked around, nobody had come for me. They led us into a house; I searched up and down the stairs, until somebody took me by the arm, gently, as if I had lost my senses. I learned that my daughter was still alive. Relieved, I collapsed onto a chair. "But she lives in the country," they said, "and there are no phones."

Flowers. A long table in a dining room. Nobody distributed anything, everyone took what they wanted directly off the plate. Opposite me were two women whose nerves could not take it. They took so much in their sudden delirium— impossible to eat it all.

And then the toilets! White, clean, with locks—and totally private. Nobody stood outside shaking the door. In the room, the beds with white sheets, one for each of us. Friendly people, who all were concerned about us.

That same evening the rush of the uncounted visitors started who wanted to know from us what had happened to their relatives. All we could say was that they would not return. From about 12, 000 people, only 130 had survived.

These strangers looked so well kept, so well fed and clothed—to our eyes. And their horror, their grief at our reports: so new, so young, so unbroken! What we had not felt for a long time still hurt them. So it was still possible...

My first free excursion. I did not look for the home I had left years ago. I looked for the "English Garden." No black and yellow sign any more, nothing was forbidden. We Jews were even allowed to use the benches again. Only there were hardly any benches any more. Nevertheless: To lie here under the trees, to breathe the fragrance of the young grass, to sleep, to gaze without a care into the sky—oh, this gave back to life what really belonged to life. This gave back strength to hope.

But like a gloomy cloud, memories still hung from the heaven of freedom. Anxious, cautiously anticipating, we dared only slowly to adjust to normal relationships with people. That would come later after we searched every stranger with a hesitating glance: Were you one of them? Did you, too, help to mock my friends, to betray them—and much more? Was the person who denounced us still alive? Yes, he still lived and now he tried to say hello. Many terrible experiences still blocked the way. But much more frequently people of all classes extended a helping hand. Some grew into lasting friendships. But when it grew dark outside, my dead ones came out of the vastness of space to my bedside. It seemed I felt their breath: Speak to the others. Do not forget us.

During the day, however, I threw myself into the active daily life with all the strength of my newly given existence.

I continued to write. My existence had a new mission.

For Elsa Bernstein,
the Person and the Poet,
in Memoriam

Before I pick up the pen to tell about you, dear Mrs. Elsa, I ask Him who in anxious, dark times let me experience the happiness of your proximity, for the power of the word, so that those, too, who were not blessed to meet you, can enfold you into their hearts and not forget you.

Elsa Bernstein, daughter of Heinrich Porges (the founder of the first choir society in Munich and friend of Liszt and Wagner), was born in Vienna in 1866, from where her parents moved to Munich when she was three. She wanted to become an actress. An eye problem put an early end to her career, despite her initial promising successes. She then turned her full attention to poetry. In 1891 she married the well-known lawyer and writer Max Bernstein. Her main works, published by S. Fischer under the pseudonym Ernst Rosmer, are dramas—*We Three, Twilight, Mother Maria, Nausikaa, Maria Arndt*—and what became an all-time favorite, the text to Humperdinck's opera *The King's Children*. Widowed, she saw her children leave Munich—she stayed in the city, where she had her circle of friends and her work—until the summer of 1942, when, totally blind, together with her sister, she too was deported to a concentration camp. Her sister became a victim of the deprivations after a few weeks. Mrs. Elsa herself, because of her service in the arts, was sent to the so-called "House for Prominent People" (where some insignificant relief was granted); she survived miraculously and after the end of the war, at age seventy-eight, moved to Hamburg, to join her daughter, where she died a few years later.

It had stopped raining. The sun sent slanting good-byes through the window. Sitting on my bundle, hungry and fighting the aftereffects of difficult pneumonia, I scribbled some thoughts, words, sentences on a scrap of packing paper. I had no courage left. Why fight? Why endure! It was stronger than we…

Then—the door opened; an old lady came toward me: "You are to go to Elsa Bernstein. And bring your poems. She is interested in your work."

I opened my eyes wide. To Elsa Bernstein! I—with my verses, my stutterings! Then I closed my eyes again for a short moment. Elsa Bernstein had sent for me! It was really true.

I had experienced her once—at a visit in the "House for

Prominent People." How the entertainment had turned into conversation under her enthusiastic guidance! And I had left as though floating on air. This short half hour had been sufficient to joyfully convince me that they could not really destroy us. Spirit would always be stronger than force, yes, even stronger than death.

I rummaged through my little bag, searched for my best work, and the next day, after finishing work, I went to see Elsa Bernstein.

She sat, leaning against the sunlit evening wall, tall and thin, in a dark lodencape, with folded hands, totally immersed in herself. Her lids had closed over her extinguished suns, and gentle, peaceful seriousness gathered her quiet features into calm resignation. Yet a strange, sweet energy radiated from her face: It was as if the blind woman listened devotedly to music which played and flowed only inside of her. I hardly dared to disturb her.

That's when she turned toward me: "Who is there?" I introduced myself. And quickly her being, lightly touched, blossomed into lively affection. A pleasing, deep voice invited me with a slightly solemn earnestness to sit down. I sat down, started to read—and then was startled by that blessed little experience, which I would receive as a gift every time I read to her: Mrs. Elsa bowed her head in an inimitable gesture—never before and never again has ever a person listened to me like that—her head to the side, her ear toward me, her features gathered together—and this trusting energy, which she showed me, encouraged me, destroyed all my inhibitions.

197

And Mrs. Elsa knew how to give courage. Not a word about her own person, about her own successes and work from the past! She faced a new task: to bring out in the person who trusted her with her own beginnings all her existing talent. Clairvoyant, the gentle poet was able to grasp even the last hidden difficulties of what had been said, meanings which almost evaded expression in words. She just nodded or with a simple word, a little sigh she let me know how well she understood. I, however, began to see the world with new eyes, to hear it with new ears. In the midst of our exile, in the midst of death and despair, out of the fullness of her heart and because of the joyful giving of this suffering old lady, about whose health we were constantly concerned, a source of light opened up for me. Repeatedly the deprivations afflicted her heart. But she did not give up. Usually she sat next to her bed and her fine-boned, boyish hands followed with the tips of the fingers the braille script in a huge book, the weight of which she could barely handle. At times she was so deep in thought that one had to "wake" her. Then, however, she inundated her visitor with affection. To make her guest happy, her hands dug into her box for a cookie or a piece of toast which she had saved despite her own hunger. She let others talk; she was interested in everything—her way of listening stimulated creativity. Her sympathy was so pure, so joyfully fresh and without deceit. I had become a part of her existence, and even the smallest of my successes filled her with pride. Even during the most difficult times, there was no spiritual, no psychological weariness; and blindness, hunger, and illness proved to be insignificant when she could attend a musical or poetical evening entertainment, which in this camp, more than in any others—this satanic camp so full of contrasts—were legendary. The cramped space around her bed became a meeting place for the many who were looking for refuge and comfort in the realm of the spirit—and who found it there.

Only when the talk turned to her sister, so sadly lost, did her blind eyes fill with tears, and more than once she assured me of her intention, should she survive, to dedicate a memorial tablet to the deceased.

Blessed are my memories of our short walks together in front of the house and in the shadow of the huge acacia trees. I was allowed to lend her my arm, to lend her my eyes, and was surprised how surely she found her way. "I can see with my feet," she said wistfully. Then she told me about her life, about books and meetings with remarkable people. And because of her power of language and her remarkable memory and original point of view, it all took on a life of its own. Yet the goodness of her heart prevented her from having real insight into the abyss of the political happenings. Her uncomprehending disbelief was naive: "No, that is impossible. People cannot be so evil!" Only from the retrospective view of her later letters did an understanding become visible, which, extending far beyond her own experience, revealed the vision, the historical cause and effect, and the synthesizing view of a great spirit.

When I bade her farewell—it was after our liberation in June 1945—our last conversation absorbed more of my time than I had to spare and one more time it illuminated for me the deep religiosity of this genuinely sincere soul. Her parting words were in regard to my future creativity: "And—write *only* when it is tearing up your insides! For *that* will be good!"

Only much later did I find the opportunity to read *The King's Children*. There arose again before me Mrs. Elsa's being, with the poetic transparency, the balletlike ease of handling language and the multiplicity of images. The ever-present richness of her imagination did not allow for a moment of fatigue. As she lived and affected us, creating out of an abundance of images, so does her work live and affect us.

She remained my teacher to the end. Many letters went back and forth between Hamburg and Munich. In order to put her thoughts to paper independently, the blind woman learned to type in her old age. "To write poetry," she wrote, "means to compromise, to lift *it* out of an intermediate stage between being and consciousness, to form *it* intentionally!"— and in one of her last letters, in judging a prose work about my remembrances of camp: "What you say about those of us who returned home should be very slight. For we did not gain a victory. The victors are those who were murdered defenselessly in the gas chambers. To engrave their names into the black tablet of memory is surely one of the best tasks for the talent suffering has awakened in you..."

In these words Mrs. Elsa lives and bears eternal witness that humility is the true source of all greatness.

Memories of
Dr. Julius Spanier

Dr. Julius Spanier, born on April 18, 1880 in Munich, stud-
ied medicine at Ludwig-Maximilian University, settled in
Munich as a pediatrician, founded the City Welfare Department for Infants together with Professor Hecker, fought
on the western front during the First World War, and after
his return was associated with countless social activities
which he often supported with his own money. Until the
takeover of power by the National Socialists he worked as
medical examiner for the religious school of the city; he
was relieved of all official and unofficial responsibilities in
1933, lost his practice, and was exiled to the concentration
camp Theresienstadt in 1942. After he returned from there
in 1945, he was elected to the board of directors of the Jewish community and elected into the city senate, worked

from then on as head physician in the Clinic for Children on Lachner Street, and was codirector of the Society for Christian-Jewish Cooperation, where he contributed much to the understanding between Jews and Christians because of his activities and strength of personality. He died in Munich on January 27, 1959. Despite many bitter experiences, he never gave up his belief in the goodness of humanity. His motto was: "Not to partake of hate, but to partake of love, that's why I am here."

To speak about Dr. Spanier, one needs to use the simplest language. Only then can one do justice to his straightforwardness and the greatness of his being. And there is no better guide to the character of a person than his conduct during these most difficult times of trial.

It is the year 1933. At the time when the catastrophe started, a part of the Jewish people was given a certain respite. Advancing slowly, the diabolical poison gained ground only gradually. Threats and cruelties on the one hand, deceitful delays and appeasements on the other, made their victims again and again unsure, only to ultimately enmesh them in their nets more securely.

Dr. Spanier did not have the time for inner adjustment, the catching of one's breath before the eruption of hell. Far too visible, he was the focal point of society in his capacity as a first-class physician and active friend of humanity, and —not least of all—as a practicing Jew who followed the laws of his creed faithfully. No wonder that right from the start of the catastrophe they tore his official positions away from him. From one day to the next, he lost his beloved activity as school physician as well as his position with the Munich Welfare Department for Infants, whose cofounder he had been. From the beginning many of his patients, who felt obligations to the power of the state either internally or externally, stayed away. His practice shrank; Spanier was called to appear before the Internal Revenue Service: "Something is wrong here, Doctor! Why do you suddenly report such low income?" Calmly, as always, Spanier replied: "Well, gentlemen, haven't you heard of Mr. Hitler?"

It went on. The title of "doctor" was denied to all Jewish physicians. The derogatory substitute "caregiver" was put in its place. How did this wise man accept this kind of humiliation and setback? "There is nothing we can do—we'll survive somehow."

Five years passed with increasing humiliations, restrictions, and privations. The year 1938 arrived—the year of the affair Grünspan, the "Kristallnacht," the loss of apartments, the deprivation of property—the year which was already leading toward war with breathless abandonment which did not grant Jewish men a quiet hour and no longer allowed their wives respite from fear. All they could do was sit at home, wait, and pray. Many Jews from Munich were sent to Dachau. None of them returned.

On the morning of November 9, Dr. Spanier's telephone rang; at that time he still lived in Müller Street. "Save yourself, as quickly as you can! They are on their way! They are picking up everybody they can find!"

Thus he was warned. What now? "First of all, we will

have breakfast," Spanier suggests—"No!" His wife implores him: "We do not have time for breakfast!"—"At least a cup of coffee."—"No! Nothing! Let's get away!"

Then began a nervous scurrying through the labyrinth of streets. A refugee in his own hometown, which had become the innocent betrayer. On and on—they went to distant quarters in the city, where they hoped they would not be recognized, his cap deep over his face, passing watchful policemen and SA people roaming about looking for victims—on and on! The thirst became torture, they grew weaker. After all, Dr. Spanier was then close to sixty.—Quick, a cup of coffee at the train station!—No, no, we are too well known here!—Where to?

At last, it was all the same; they took a tram and rode at random to Laim. Oh, finally a tiny café, far away! Nobody knows us here, we can rest here, get some strength! They were about to enter, when at the last moment they recognized the man who was washing windows, a fanatic member of the party and enemy of Jews. They fled, as quickly as possible. It was almost noon. Where could they find shelter in this city for whose welfare he had lived, worked, and made sacrifices?

Near the *Ostbahnhof* * lived a family who had been part of his circle of patients for years. Modest, quiet citizens who knew no difference between human beings—and also no fear. When they recognized the visitors, they opened their door wide. Here at last was peace, between the sheltering walls they could breathe calmly. For a few hours, he was himself again.

---

*East station

When darkness fell, Mrs. Spanier and their host went back to their apartment and she gave him the weapons which her husband still possessed from his participation in the First World War. If they were found at his house, it would mean for him, a Jew, death. The friend left and promised to throw them into the river.

In his hiding place, Dr. Spanier trembled for his wife, who returned late that night. But they could not stay here. To hide with so-called Aryans would mean to bring their rescuers into danger. Could he take this responsibility?—Away, away! But not back home, where one could be discovered most quickly! Where to?—To the Jewish hospital. He had already transferred what was left of his practice to the hospital; he had been retained as their active physician. There he would be welcomed with open arms.

Barely had they arrived when somebody stormed breathlessly through the door: "Turn off the light! They are coming!" No respite here either. The search for victims did not stop even in a hospital.

There was an empty bed. At his wife's entreaty, he took off his clothes, pulled the blanket up to his head. He stayed there, motionless, while they searched the house. His hiding place was overlooked by the scouts. Now they were leaving. Take a deep breath—Thank God.—Two minutes later they were back. Again inspection of all rooms, stairways, and halls. Again they overlooked his room. But now Dr. Spanier could not take it any longer. He jumped up: "Enough! I am leaving! What evil thing have I done! I was in the war—I have seen other dangers! I do not need to hide here!"

Two of them held him down and locked the door, not because of the pursuers, but because of the pursued, who wanted to give himself up to his persecutors.

When the danger had passed, Spanier had his first heart spasm in his life. Then he calmly and factually concluded: "We are not safe anywhere. We are going back to our apartment."

Could one live without fear in one's own home? For weeks the search for Jewish men was continued. It meant to hide even here, as if nobody was home. It also meant no light, no water, so that no gurgling could be heard in the pipes, darkness day and night. If the telephone rang, one would not pick up the receiver, or one would have given oneself away. But how to help his patients? Pulling down his faithful cap deep over his face, Spanier went to visit his patients *at night*, while his wife used anonymous telephone booths—which she constantly changed—to find out who needed help. Poor patients, and there were many of them then, he treated free of charge; indeed, he even gave them presents.

At night the faithful brought him groceries from the *Ostbahnhof.* To go shopping himself would have been dangerous. The year drew to a close under constant anxieties.

Nineteen thirty-nine. War broke out. In the fall, out of necessity, the couple moved their lodging into the Jewish hospital. Practice and living quarters, both were together again. A bitter consolation.—"You were in the war?" asked the leader of

the battalion of the SA, "and you know how to treat people?"—"Yes, I know how."—"Then you will be the medical
examiner for the mobilization of labor from now on.—But
you will not be paid."—"I am used to that," Spanier replied.

Medical examiner for the mobilization of labor—what did
that mean? In Lohhof, between Munich and Dachau, Jews of
both genders, starting with mere children up to old age, were
forced to work in the preparation of flax. Compulsory work,
which, with respect to its requirements and personal treatment, was the most consuming kind of work designed for
brutal exploitation and invented to hasten extermination.
The old people collapsed; the young ones, under inhuman
pressure of time, lost hands in the machines and fell victim
to hunger and the ruthless pace of work. To be the medical
examiner for those people meant to carry a double burden of
responsibility, to make decisions daily and hourly between
following those "gentlemen" in command or his own conscience, and endangering himself the most. If he ordered all
sick people off work, he overdrew the quota and gave up the
possibility of freeing at least the feeblest from work for a
short while. But how could those for whom he was to care,
especially the young ones, react to this without bitterness?
Yet they accepted it; they understood their physician
because he understood their needs.

   During this activity—in the Jewish senior citizens home
in Hermann Schmid Street—a chance happening permitted

me to meet him personally for the first time. It was only for a moment, when somebody seriously injured was brought to him. Never will I forget what I read in his face. This was not common, cheap sympathy—no, this was deep, suffering compassion that sees himself in his brother.

Head physician of the hospital, private physician, medical examiner—on top of all that the order came to function also as camp physician in camp Berg am Laim, where the remaining Jews of the city were driven together. When? There was no time during the day. So—at night. How to get there? To use the tram had been forbidden long ago. To walk on foot from the Hermann Schmid Street to Berg am Laim and back, three times a week, no mortal being could possibly accomplish that. Now his cap came in handy again. But alas, added to that, and worsening the situation: the Jewish star! So Spanier hurried in darkness to the *Südbahnhof,** his writing case pressed to his chest to hide the star and his cap deep over his face, from where the night train left for Berg am Laim.

"At least they should allow physicians to drive," he announced indignantly. He spoke in front of treacherous ears. It was passed on. On a Friday morning, Spanier returned home; it was June 1942: "Honey, now you have to pack."—"What! We move again?"—"No, not this time. Transport—to Theresienstadt." Spanier was the first physician from Munich who was deported. Someone had denounced him.

Friends came; they brought groceries and bedding. However, weight and space was prescribed; it meant limiting oneself. Next day, in Camp Milbertshofen, the baggage went

---

*South station

through the so-called sluice. By the bushel basket stolen property was put aside.—"Now our suitcases are nice and light." With these words Spanier greeted his wife when he returned from the barracks. They had stolen almost everything.

In the end, a well-meaning companion offered him a surprising present: Cyanide. "You'll never know when you will need it."—"Take it back," Spanier said. "I am in God's hands. What He inflicts on me I will bear."

On the way. Burning summer heat. Order: "Who ever opens a window or sticks his head out will be shot." Spanier stuck his head out. "Close the window!" someone yelled outside. Spanier did not lose his composure. "I am responsible for caring for the sick. Part of that job is giving them water."—Another warning: "Window closed!"—"Okay, I will close it now," Spanier answered.

What would happen now? As the trip continued, he asked himself: Will they shoot me when the train stops? Or will I stay alive? The train stopped. A voice yelled into the window. "Now you can have water!" Spanier's courage had impressed them. The perplexed SS officer even worked the pump handle to help the nurses fill the pitchers.

Theresienstadt. A member of the Council of Elders meets the well-known physician with the offer to secure a privileged place for him, his own room, and better food, because of his past services. Spanier refuses everything: "I always wanted just once to be only a physician without pay. I do not want to be privileged here, I only want to help."

This attitude probably saved his life. Theresienstadt was not the end of the road. The notion, which many people had, that here after many years of torture and fear they would find peace, was based on the deceitful promises of the Gestapo officials. Theresienstadt meant hunger, cold, epidemics, tight space, and vermin, scarcity of even the most primitive civilized accommodations—wholesale deaths and unending fear of transport. Theresienstadt was a reservoir before the next transport into the death chambers of Auschwitz. And the more prominent, the more exposed. But who thought about that! Only after it was too late did the poor victim realize that it would have been better not to be considered prominent. The fear of transport terrorized everybody—until the last day. At night we would lie on the floor, one next to the other, freezing, wasted from hunger, and yet wishing for the day and for forced labor in order to forget.

"Well, Doctor," an acquaintance asked, "how do you like Theresienstadt?" Spanier's answer: "What do you want—here we have no telephone, no internal revenue, no administrative authorities, I do not have to send out bills—why shouldn't I like it?"

A physician in Theresienstadt. Yes, there were many good doctors. But what good did it do: there was no medicine. Daily up to 170 people died in camp. Physician in the house for youth—nice. Young people especially fell victim in large numbers to epidemics, and children-only transports were even sent to the death camp of Auschwitz.

Spanier let nobody know when his heart was heavy. He

always seemed cheerful, told funny anecdotes. His humor helped the seriously ill to forget their suffering for a while. Everybody called him "sunshine."

"Behold, the guardian of Israel neither sleeps nor naps."* Spanier used this Bible citation—quoted by Cardinal Faulhaber to console the Munich Rabbi Baerwald—to console his patients now. Often he was not only their physician, but their spiritual advisor as well, and he always carried his little black cap in his pocket, so that he could say the prayers for the dead over the departing, since rarely was a rabbi about.

Despite deprivation and overwork from the treatment of the ill, he took an intense interest in the study of illnesses occurring in camp. It was he who recognized a prevailing mysterious illness among prisoners: pellagra. He then held several lectures for his colleagues to inform them about the cause, nature, and method of treatment. The latter came to naught—again because of lack of medicine. It did not take him long to diagnose his own wife's illness; she had all the symptoms of pellagra. She also could not be helped. There simply was nothing available.

That for three long years all transports bypassed the couple is one of the miracles of Theresienstadt—but then, every survivor is a miracle.

At last the day arrived. Theresienstadt was liberated by the Russians. For the time being, however, we did not experience much freedom, though life became easier, hunger stopped, hope sprang up again. But the so-called death

---

*Psalm 121:4

marches just before the end, which herded together people from many different camps and drove them to Theresienstadt, had brought with them typhoid. The result was chaos. The number of physicians had been reduced, but the number of patients grew daily. At times, doctors and nurses worked three days and nights without interruption to give even the most primitive help, and the weeks passed with a feverish effort to achieve the highest performance. At the head: Dr. Spanier.

His activity was soon put to an end: "I think I have typhoid," he said one morning, but got up anyway and tried to go to work. He collapsed on the spot. He had been right in his diagnosis. Luckily, he had been vaccinated; otherwise he would not have survived. I visited him. Tortured by pain, weakened by fever, and in spite of the uncertain outcome, he appeared cheerful, kindly, and fatherly, just as I had always known him.

Though he survived the typhoid, his heart was permanently damaged. Not until August 1945, lying in an ambulance, did the patient return home in one of the last transfers to the city of his fathers—almost two months later than most of the surviving prisoners.

Never will I forget the day when Spanier was elected president of the Jewish community in Munich. It happened shortly after his return, as unceremoniously as possible, and took place in the senior citizens home in Kaulbach Street, which had miraculously survived the bombing attacks. After the official part was over, the newly elected went for a walk in the garden. He saw me sitting there on a bench, reunited with my little family, and coming over to us, without wasting many words on greetings, he put his hand on top of the baby's head to feel for fontanels. Then, again without saying a word, he pulled out his prescription pad and wrote out a prescription. He did not want to hear about gratitude.

How was life to go on after all the horrors which had happened? Very simple: One buries all bitterness; love for humanity is stronger, passion for the profession unbroken. "I have forgotten everything," he used to say gently. But I never believed him. The Jew in him could not, should not, and did not want to forget. But his kind heart had *forgiven*, and his farseeing spirit growing *out* of experience *transcended* the experience. After the war, in his capacity as president of the Chamber of Physicians he had the difficult task of informing some of his colleagues that because of their political past they would not be allowed to practice. "You see," he consoled them, "life has its ups and downs. It happened to me, too, and as for me, so for you, too, things will change again, some day." He helped a woman physician, the wife of a colleague who because of his political past had to spend time in Camp Moosburg, to open an office so that she could support herself and her child. Never had he met such a person, her husband exclaimed when he heard about it.

Times change, but they could not change the man. Neither could high honors make him proud, nor disappointments embitter him. For the companions of those difficult days of common sufferings, he always remained the helping, understanding friend. Whoever entered his house entered into a house of peace. Whoever met him met a father.

Never did he take an honorarium from his friends and companions in suffering. We were all defenseless before this, his great goodness. And one other small, highly esteemed characteristic: When Dr. Spanier examined his patients—he probably was not even aware of it—he was in the habit of addressing them with "*du*," even if at other times he addressed them with "*Sie.*" He was the father, and gladly one was his child.

Without doubt, this wonderful friend of humanity would have lived longer had not the horrors of the persecutions inflicted irreversible injury on his heart. A few days before his death I visited him for the last time. He was fully aware of his condition. All the love and faithfulness of his colleagues could not deter the course of the illness. With high honors he was buried and mourned.

A well-known proverb says that men are replaceable. Julius Spanier is a convincing example of the shortsightedness of this proverb, and of the reality that each person in his totality is an irrecoverable manifestation and a unique event.